# Slave and Citizen

## *The Life of Frederick Douglass*

*Nathan Irvin Huggins*

# Slave and Citizen

## *The Life of Frederick Douglass*

*Edited by Oscar Handlin*

Scott, Foresman and Company
Glenview, Illinois   London, England

Printed in the United States of America.

ISBN 0-673-39342-9

789101112131415-PAT-98979695949392919089

HAL

*for Louise Dean Smith and John Fletcher Smith*

# Editor's Preface

By 1841, many Bostonians and some New Englanders in other parts of the United States had become abolitionists. They considered the South's peculiar institution incompatible with the republican nature of their country. In an era of progress, slavery was an anachronistic heritage of the past, incompatible with the Christian belief that all men were perfectible. Evangelical Protestants and secular believers in reform alike accepted the obligation to hasten the day of the extinction of human bondage. These were the abstract ideas of well-intentioned, bookish men and women, very few of whom had actually seen a slave or had more than secondhand contact with the institution of slavery. Not many indeed had had much to do with any black people.

Hence the impression Frederick Douglass made upon the audience to which he spoke at the Nantucket Atheneum in August 1841. Here a man, not an abstraction but a creature of flesh and blood. Not long before, he had been a chattel, a thing bought and sold. But the escape to freedom had restored his manhood so that now he addressed the meeting in meaningful terms using the intellectual equipment acquired through his own efforts.

The abolitionists took up Douglass, who seemed the crowning evidence to complete their case; then for years he labored in the effort to persuade others. In so doing, he entered into the mainstream of the reform movements that occupied increasing attention of Americans in the decades before 1860.

The Civil War only broadened these opportunities, for those who believed in black equality, as Douglass did, had to present that case to President Lincoln and even more convincingly to the commanders of the Union army. The effort to do so culminated in the Emancipation Proclamation and completed the first phase of Frederick Douglass's life.

The end of slavery, however, opened up a second and different phase. Reform, in the pre–Civil War sense of the term, proved inadequate to deal either with the problems of blacks or with the complexities of the new society that emerged as the nineteenth century drew to a close. An urban, industrial society then presented the citizens of the republic with unprecedented challenges, and neither Douglass nor the rest of the country knew how to grapple with them. The tools inherited from an earlier, simpler culture proved inadequate to the task. The life of this man thus illustrates the dilemmas of a painful transition in the nation's history.

OSCAR HANDLIN

# Contents

# Slave and Citizen
## *The Life of Frederick Douglass*

# I

# In Every Man the Spark

IN EARLY AUGUST 1841 an antislavery convention met on Nantucket Island. William C. Coffin, a New Bedford abolitionist, called upon a young black man from that town to stand and tell his story. Frederick Douglass stood and addressed the crowd. He was an arresting figure, in his early twenties, over six feet in height, robust in frame, forceful and direct in manner. He was physically attractive, but it was what he had to say that galvanized his audience.

He had escaped just three years before from slavery, was a fugitive in the North, and even now was subject to capture and forced return to bondage in the South. He gave detailed observations about life as a slave, verifying the suspicions and fears of an audience with no firsthand knowledge of slavery.

When Douglass took his seat, his listeners were deeply moved. William Lloyd Garrison then followed with an inspired lecture on the evils and corruption of the system which would use a man like Frederick Douglass as if he were a brute. He reminded members of the convention that it was not merely Southern society and slaveholders who were corrupt, but the law, the government, and the churches that sustained the system. No less corrupt were those individuals who, by their complacency and indifference, gave assent to the crime of "man stealing." Garrison reminded them that Douglass and all fugitive slaves were in peril even in Massachusetts. Would they, he asked, allow this man to be carried back to slavery, "law or no law, constitution or no constitution"? Their response was a thunderous "No."

Thus, Frederick Douglass was welcomed into the antislavery movement. As the Nantucket convention ended, John A. Collins asked Douglass to be a speaker for the Massachusetts Anti-Slavery Society. He had only to travel with Stephen S. Foster and tell his story as he had just done. The society would pay him $450 a year, just slightly more than he could earn as a common laborer in New Bedford. Douglass agreed, and began a lifelong career as speaker and publicist in the cause of black Americans.

Douglass was a powerful addition to the abolitionists, attractive and well-spoken, but his greatest asset was the story he told. Most of the blacks who spoke from abolitionist platforms were free persons, and even those who had once been slaves had gained their freedom by purchase or manumission. Frederick Douglass, however, had escaped, was a fugitive still, and but for his master's ignorance of his whereabouts would be at once returned to slavery. Douglass's story therefore was even more fascinating because he stood in defiance of the law, and because the telling of it took a rare kind of courage. Here, too, was a message not to be lost on those whites who thought of blacks as craven and unmanly.

For four years Douglass told fragments of his life story, guarding always the details of names, places, and means of escape which might have identified him to his master and exposed friends and accomplices who had helped him on his way.

The role destiny played in when and how he gained his freedom intrigued Douglass as it did his listeners. There must have been a time while still in the thralldom of slavery when he knew he must be free, from which moment his escape was inevitable. Was that not a sign that the spirit of freedom was latent in every man? Did not his life justify faith in human potentialities? What would it all imply for those still enthralled? He would ponder such questions for years to come.

By the end of his life Frederick Douglass had written three autobiographies, telling what he knew and could remember of family and friends, slave and free. The details were slow to appear, revealed gradually, as he thought it safe to do so. Each autobiography varied a bit the one preceding it, as time and circumstances called for different emphases—but all had a common theme. They each told the story of a public not a private life, of a man whose story ought to dispel ignorance and prejudice about blacks. His autobiographies showed the true character of his people as well as the evils of slavery and the system of racial oppression that followed emanicipation. Rightly understood, his life would be the most powerful argument for racial justice. His life, as Douglass saw it from the very beginning of his public career, exemplified something much greater than his private self. What was possible for him was also potential within other black men and women. Furthermore, it revealed in him—a black man, a slave, the man farthest down—the spark of liberty, of humanity, of what some would call divinity. Through the story of this life one could glimpse human potentialities, and indeed human perfectibility, a testament for an American faith.

As were most slaves, Frederick Douglass was ignorant of the most elementary facts of his birth. He remained uncertain of his birthdate, but he was born in 1818 near Easton, in Talbot County, Maryland. His mother was Harriet Bailey, daughter of Isaac, a freeman, and Betsey Bailey. He was told his own father was a white man, but he never learned the man's identity. He was named Frederick Augustus Washington Bailey.

Because his mother did, Douglass also belonged to Aaron Anthony, owner of about thirty slaves and three farms. Anthony also managed about a thousand slaves belonging to Colonel Edward Lloyd. Harriet Bailey's work for Anthony did not permit her to care for her own children. So Frederick grew up in the cabin of his grandparents, and his mother had to walk several miles after her work to visit him. She died while he was still young, leaving him only vague memories of fugitive visits in the night.

Betsey Bailey, the only real mother Frederick knew, had five daughters whose children when small were left in her care. Besides being a good nurse, she made nets for catching shad and herring, was a good fisherwoman and gardener, and had a special gift for cultivating seedling yams. She had a somewhat privileged status, not only among slaves, but with Aaron Anthony. He left her to her own cabin with no responsibilities other than the care of her grandchildren and herself.

Frederick, as a small child, led a rather carefree life in his grandmother's cabin, but when he was about seven he felt for the first time the bitter reality of slavery. Without telling him why, Betsey Bailey took Frederick to Aaron Anthony's place. It was twelve miles, a long walk for the little boy, so his grandmother "toted" him on her shoulders part of the way. There were other children there, and his grandmother made Frederick play with them. They are "kin to you," she told him, and so for the first time he met his half brother and four half sisters. While he played, his grandmother left the place, and Frederick was never as a child to see her again. Thus ended his only real attachment to family.

His brief stay at the Anthony place affected him deeply. There he saw floggings for the first time and later would remember the especially brutal treatment of his Aunt Hester at the hands of Captain Anthony. Other episodes clung to his mind long afterward as examples of the brutalizing nature of slavery. He remembered a cousin who walked over ten miles to show her master wounds incurred in a beating by an overseer. She got little sympathy. Her master merely forced her to return to the overseer, threatening another beating if she did not obey. The slave was conditioned to violence and, as Douglass was to recall, this often made slaves mean and insensitive to one another.

In 1825 good fortune came to Frederick. He was sent to Baltimore to live in the household of Hugh and Sophia Auld as the companion to their son, Tommy. It was a crucial move in that not only were the Aulds reasonably kind, but he was to live during his formative years in an urban setting. The city was to shape him and give him his first glimpse of freedom.

Frederick's education began by learning to read. He persuaded Mrs. Auld, a pious and gentle woman, to teach him to read the Bible. He was an apt student and with his mistress as tutor quickly learned the alphabet and the spellings of words of three or four letters. Sophia Auld's innocence betrayed her, however. She proudly showed her husband how good a teacher she was and how quickly and well the slave boy could learn. Hugh Auld was not at all pleased—in fact he was enraged.

Hugh Auld, with coarse and brutal language, told his wife that slaves should never be taught beyond their station. Not only was it illegal to teach them to read, but it would "spoil the best n[igge]r in the world." A slave, "given an inch, he will take an ell," he said. A slave should know nothing but the will of his master. "If you learn him how to read, he'll want to know how to write; and, this accomplished, he'll be running away with himself."

Hugh Auld's lecture made an important impression on both Sophia Auld and Frederick Bailey. She never again, in the seven years he remained in her household, attempted to teach him anything that might cause him to want to elevate his condition. Frederick, on the other hand, learned the most important lesson of his youth: there was something unnatural about slavery; he was a slave not because he was incapable of better but because he was deprived of the means. Hugh Auld had made it clear that reading and writing were more than mere skills. They were the way out of slavery. Frederick was more determined than ever to learn the forbidden.

With seriousness of purpose, Frederick plotted his education as if it were an intrigue, enlisting knowing and unknowing conspirators. He bribed, coaxed, and tricked white boys into sharing their lessons with him. When he began to work as an unskilled laborer in the Baltimore shipyards, he converted the signs and symbols used by carpenters and craftsmen into lessons for the shaping of letters. He tried to read everything that came into his hands, including the vagrant scraps of newspapers he found in the Baltimore streets. When he was thirteen, having taught himself, and having managed to get fifty cents, he bought his first book, *The Columbian Orator.*

He had overheard some boys say they must learn some pieces from that book, so he moved quickly to own and study it. It was a standard school book for rhetoric, containing brief speeches by famous orators as well as dialogues to be practiced and memorized. The exercises taught the declamatory style of the times, also teaching virtues such as honesty, diligence, and courage. They proclaimed the inevitable triumph of truth and reason over ignorance and passion. Frederick would always remember reading the speeches of champions of liberty and human rights: Richard Brinsley Sheridan, Charles James Fox, and the younger William Pitt. He was especially impressed by a speech for Catholic emancipation by Daniel O'Connell and a dialogue in which a slave, by careful reason, convinced his master of the immorality of slavery and of his duty to set him free.

Hugh Auld was right; education would spoil a person for slavery. But reading was not the only danger. The streets of the city were educational, too. Frederick learned to argue his case with his white boyhood companions. They looked forward to growing up because once they came of age, they could do as they pleased. They would be free from the wardship of childhood. Frederick saw the unfairness in this. As an adult he was to remain the ward and property of another. He witnessed the miserable condition of some slaves, treated like animals by their masters. He met free blacks and learned of a condition other than his own. Some he met were sailors from ships visiting Baltimore's port, and he heard from them of Northern cities—free cities—like Philadelphia, New York, and Boston. Also on the docks he saw the coffles of slaves being shipped by boat to Southern markets, from which it seemed there could be no return, no possible escape. Newspapers, like the *Baltimore American,* fell into his hands, and from them he learned about abolitionists and their agitation against slavery. He read of Nat Turner's insurrection in Virginia, and he sensed an unspoken fear on the part of the Southern journalists who reported these matters. The feeling began to grow on him that the evil he had come to know as slavery was already in the throes of divine retributive justice.

In Baltimore, too, Frederick was awakened to a religious spirit. The preachings of a white Methodist made the slave boy feel the sinful character of all men, who could be reconciled with God only through Christ. A black man named Charles Johnson, taught Frederick that the human heart—slave or free—could be changed by "casting all one's cares upon God." And the loving devotion of an old black man named Lawson, whom he called "Father," convinced Frederick that he would be free if only he really wanted it and relied on God. The old man told him the "Lord had a great work for me to do, and I must prepare to do it." Although Hugh Auld forbade him to, Frederick met with "Father" Lawson often, especially on Sundays when they held devotions together. They continued the relationship—surreptitious father and son—until the boy was forced to return to the country.

Frederick must have been heartbroken to learn of the death of his master, not because of any fondness for the man but for the change it meant to his own life. Aaron Anthony died in 1831 when Frederick was thirteen. The boy had to return to the plantation to await the reading of the dead man's will. There could be no telling what might happen. He might be sold away to settle some outstanding debt, he could become the property of one of the heirs, or he might be returned to the household of Hugh Auld. As it turned out, he was fortunate. He became the property of Lucretia Anthony Auld, the daughter of his former master, whom he remembered as having been kind to him during his previous stay on the plantation. She was kind once again, allowing the boy to return to her brother-in-law's home in Baltimore.

In this settlement of the dead man's estate, however, Betsey Bailey, Frederick's grandmother, did not fare so well. The old woman, now decrepit, was put in a cabin in the woods and, as the boy saw it, left to die.

Within a year, Lucretia Auld and her brother Andrew were dead, making Frederick now the property of Lucretia's husband, Thomas. Two years after Lucretia's death, Thomas Auld remarried a woman who owned an estate near St. Michaels, Maryland, where he now established himself. These changes need not have affected Frederick except that the brothers, Thomas and Hugh, had a serious disagreement, and Thomas demanded that Frederick be returned to him. Thus, at fifteen, Frederick was forced again to cut his ties with the city and return to country life. This time it seemed it would be a permanent move.

How much resentment Frederick felt, having been forced to leave the city, we do not know. Part of a slave's education was to learn to repress anger. The city boy, however, had experienced a liberty of thought and action wholly alien to a country slave's imagination. Moreover, he could read and write, which at once made him exceptional among the slaves at St. Michaels.

The boy continued to take his sense of a calling seriously, but was frustrated as there was little in the way of religious instruction for slaves or free blacks. When a black man named Wilson asked Frederick to assist him in teaching a Sabbath school, the boy jumped at the chance. The class met at a freeman's house, where there were a dozen old spelling books and a few Bibles for the twenty hopeful scholars. It was an exhilarating experience, and Frederick thought he had found a way of helping his people. The second meeting, however, was broken up by a mob of white men from the town—led by Thomas Auld.

The effort to establish a Sabbath school probably convinced

Thomas Auld that Frederick was likely to give him trouble unless he was disciplined. He hired the boy to a small farmer named Edward Covey, who had a reputation for conditioning slaves to the hard labor of the farm. He rented his land and was able to hire slaves cheaply because of his reputation for "breaking them in."

In his sixteenth year, Frederick had achieved full physical growth and could be expected to do the work of a full hand in the fields. From January to December 1834, he was under Covey's charge. He not only learned the tough physical labors of the farm but, for the first time in his life, he came to know the pain and humiliation of the lash. Frederick doubtless was a bit independent and somewhat arrogant, and Covey was a mean man who saw his task as bending the boy's will and converting him into a good, obedient slave. Frederick was beaten almost daily. Ironically, it was this effort to reduce the boy to submission that provoked him to assert himself in a defiant way for the first time.

He had already suffered six months from Covey's blows when the crisis came. On a very hot summer's day, he fell ill while working in the fields. Covey accused him of feigning, kicked him, and cut his head with a blow from a wooden plank. Frederick ran off, losing Covey in the woods, and headed back to St. Michaels. He hoped that Thomas Auld, seeing his condition, would take him back from Covey. He was mistaken. Auld accused him of having been at fault; to take the boy back would have meant forfeiting a year's wages that Covey had paid. Auld told the boy to stay overnight but to return to Covey in the morning.

Wending his way back the next morning, Frederick was perplexed as to how to avoid facing Covey and the beating he would surely get for having run away. He hid out in the woods near Covey's farm for the whole day and on into the night. Covey, knowing that hunger would sooner or later compel the boy to return, felt no need to hunt him down.

At night, in the woods, a slave named Sandy came upon

Frederick. Sandy was headed to the house of his wife—a freewoman—to spend the Sabbath with her. Despite the risk to himself and his wife, he persuaded Frederick to come with him so that they could eat and figure out a solution to the boy's problem. They talked into the early hours of the morning.

Sandy was something of a conjurer, boasting of power from African sources to cure and to curse. He told Frederick of a root, common in the neighborhood, that he would give him, and that if he wore it on his right side, no white person would whip him. Although Frederick thought of all this as superstitious and absurd if not "positively sinful," he did wear the root as Sandy directed when he returned to Covey on Sunday morning.

His stay in the woods and the long talk with Sandy and his wife had no doubt helped him resolve something in his mind, for he confronted Covey quite fearlessly. Since it was the Sabbath, Covey did not touch him or raise his voice in anger.

Monday, however, was a different story. Covey attempted to beat Frederick, and the boy resisted. They wrestled in the cowyard, the boy simply holding the white man and telling him that he would not be beaten again. The other workers refused to help Covey. So convinced that he could not subdue the boy by force, Covey released him. However Covey rationalized it, he did not attempt to whip Frederick Bailey for the rest of the year. Some part of the boy was no longer a slave.

When Frederick finished his year with Covey, Thomas Auld hired him out to another neighbor. He was to spend two years on the farm of William Freeland, a much gentler man than Covey. Frederick was obliged to work hard, but he was fed well and no attempt was made to beat him. His experiences with Covey, however, had made him even more determined not to remain a slave. He began a secret school in the woods, teaching reading and the Bible to slaves and free blacks in the neighborhood. By the end of the first year he had forty students.

The raid on his Sabbath school had been fair warning to Frederick. Educating blacks was a subversive enterprise. Secrecy, however, engendered a spirit of conspiracy, and it was not long before Frederick and five other slaves were plotting an escape to freedom.

Their scheme was to steal a boat and take off on the eve of the Easter holiday, rowing as fast as they could to cover the seventy miles to the head of the Chesapeake Bay. There, they would abandon the boat and set out on foot, following the North Star into Pennsylvania. Frederick wrote passes for himself and his five comrades, hoping that these would get them by whites who might stop them along the way.

Whites learned of their plot, however, and the day they were to leave the conspirators were rounded up by armed deputies and marched to St. Michaels where they were questioned. They were then taken fifteen miles to jail in Easton. The band of conspirators had managed to dispose of their passes before they reached St. Michaels, and as each steadfastly denied any knowledge of a plot, there was not enough evidence to convict them. So they were released to their masters.

Thomas Auld remained suspicious of Frederick. He was certain that the boy had been somehow engaged in a scheme to escape. He decided to send him away from St. Michaels, for the boy's reputation in the neighborhood would make his hire difficult. Auld was tempted to sell Frederick to one of the traders who marketed slaves in the deep South, but he had a change of heart. Having made up his differences with his brother Hugh, he agreed to send Frederick back to Baltimore. He told the boy that if he learned a trade and avoided getting into trouble, he would free him when he reached twenty-five.

It was more than Frederick Bailey could have hoped for. He was returning to Baltimore and the relative freedom he had known there, and he could look forward to becoming a free man in seven years if Auld kept his word. He was immediately put to work in the shipyards, where he learned the caulker's trade.

It was as a skilled worker that he learned a new dimension of racism and an ironic twist of slavery. The white workers at the shipyards, through violence and threats of work stoppage, forced free black workers out of the yards. White men refused to compete with black workers. As a slave and the property of a white man, Frederick was somewhat protected. Nevertheless, he was assaulted by a gang of white apprentices who hoped to force him off the job. Despite such violence, Frederick became an expert caulker and by 1838 was earning the highest wage paid for that work. His earnings, of course, went to Hugh Auld, and that increased his resentment of his condition.

He persuaded Hugh Auld to allow him to work on his own. They agreed that Frederick would seek out and bargain for his own employment, buy his own tools and clothing, and pay three dollars a week to Auld. The rest of his earnings he could keep for himself. At the going rate, that meant that he would work two days for Hugh Auld and whatever else he could earn during the week was his own. At the same time, Auld was relieved of much of the expense for Frederick's upkeep. It was a new stage on the way to freedom for Frederick, and he took to it well, earning far more than he had when Auld had to find him places and had taken all of his earnings.

Hugh Auld had been right when he admonished his wife that "given an inch," Frederick would "take an ell." Small increments of freedom made Frederick Bailey even more restive. Earning money for himself made all the more tangible what he paid weekly to Hugh Auld. What could justify such an exploitation of his labor? His resentment grew stronger rather than abating, and he pressed even harder against the limits on his freedom.

Taking advantage of the liberty the city afforded, Frederick joined such self-help associations as the East Baltimore Improvement Society where he met with other blacks, slave and free, to debate, learn and plot.

Anna Murray became one of his closest friends. She was freeborn, about eight years his senior, one of twelve children of Bambara and Mary Murray. She had left her home in Denton, Maryland, when she was eighteen, coming to Baltimore where she worked as a housekeeper for a well-to-do family. Frederick and Anna grew very close and planned to marry. But these plans made Frederick's slavery all the more burdensome. Anna encouraged him in what had become an obsession to escape. She gave him her meager savings from over nine years' work.

Frederick's greater sense of independence and his resolve to take his own destiny into his hands made him more daring. One summer weekend in 1838, Frederick took it upon himself to go to an all-night camp meeting. He found it inconvenient to ask Hugh Auld's permission or to give him his three dollars before leaving. Auld was enraged. When Frederick returned, Auld predicted that he would try to escape if things continued the way they were. He took away all of Frederick's newly won privileges so that he was now obliged to turn over all of his earnings to Auld, and he would have to ask permission whenever he wanted to be away from the house.

It was Frederick's turn for anger. In retaliation he did not seek work the following week and came on Saturday to Hugh Auld with empty hands; if they were back to the old arrangement, Hugh Auld would have to find him work. This "strike" so angered Auld that the two nearly came to blows. Frederick realized, however, that he could not risk a fight that might cause him to be sent away from Baltimore and make his escape from slavery nearly impossible. He was now convinced that he had to escape at the earliest opportunity, but that resolve made it imperative that his behavior be above Hugh Auld's reproach. So he turned dutifully to work, giving his earnings each week to Auld, and taking whatever small change the white man cared to give him as a gratuity.

Among Frederick's friends were some of the black sailors who worked the ships frequenting Baltimore's port. They carried seamen's papers which they used instead of the freedom papers Southern free blacks were obliged to carry. Frederick borrowed the papers of one of his friends, promising to return them by mail once he got to a Northern city.

On Monday, 3 September, 1838, Frederick Bailey hopped on the back of a train as it pulled out of the Baltimore station heading for Philadelphia. He was wearing sailor's clothing and carrying the papers of his friend. It was an anxious journey, and all the way North he expected to be recognized at any moment. He was afraid that the conductor might look closely at the papers he carried and see that he did not resemble the description on them. The train reached Wilmington, Delaware, without his exposure as an impostor. From there, he took a steamer to Philadelphia. The first and perhaps the hardest part of his escape was a success. He was in the North, where having a black face did not automatically dub one a slave. He had to put more distance between himself and his master, so he took the first chance to go to New York City.

Northern cities like Philadelphia and New York were by no means safe for fugitives. Frederick Bailey was worth money and soon there would be a bounty for his return. Most white men, and some blacks, would turn him over to authorities if they suspected he was a fugitive. If he were caught now, it could mean that he would be sold to someone in the deep South and lose whatever chance for freedom he might have had.

Having no friends, he wandered the streets of New York for several days. He was afraid to speak to anyone, afraid to look for work, afraid that anybody could tell his secret merely by looking at him. At last, he took courage and spoke to a black sailor, telling him his plight. The sailor directed him to the home of David Ruggles, a black abolitionist and secretary of the New York Vigilance Committee.

Ruggles put him up in his home, and he was soon joined by Anna Murray. On September 15 Reverend James W. C. Pennington, who had himself ten years earlier fled a Maryland master, married Frederick and Anna. But New York was not the best place for a fugitive slave to settle, and plans were quickly made for the couple to move on.

Ruggles suggested that they go to New Bedford, Massachusetts. It was safer, there was more antislavery sentiment than in New York, and agents of slaveholders were far less likely to go there. It was also a whaling port with a considerable amount of shipbuilding work. It was thought that Frederick could easily find employment following his trade. The couple followed Ruggles's advice. Nathan Johnson, a black abolitionist in New Bedford, took Frederick and Anna in and helped them to get started on their new life.

One of the first problems the freeman faced was getting a new name. While Frederick Augustus Washington Bailey had managed to "steal" himself, he was still legally the property of Thomas Auld. He could be brought before United States courts and forcibly returned. While he could not disguise himself, he could at least rid himself of a name that might make it easier to trace him and which was associated in his mind with his life as a slave. It was mere coincidence that he chose the name Douglass. Nathan Johnson had been reading Sir Walter Scott's *Lady of the Lake* and was moved by the character in that novel. So Frederick and Anna started their new life, in a new town, with a new name.

It was not so simple a matter for Frederick Douglass to pick up his trade in New Bedford. There was work enough for skilled caulkers, but he was to learn another irony of race relations in the United States. While a slave, one could follow a craft for the benefit of a master, but as a free black man one was not allowed to compete with white labor. That had been true in Baltimore, and it was no less true in New Bedford. White men assumed a privilege, a preference in all lines of work, and a right to exclude blacks from desirable trades. New Bedford caulkers, like the white craftsmen in Baltimore, would refuse to work if a black man was hired on the job.

To make a living, Douglass was forced to pick up odd jobs as a common laborer. He took this setback rather amiably, so pleased was he to be free and his own boss. He found a lot of work—shoveling coal, sawing wood, working bellows for furnaces in the mills. This kind of work did not pay much, but they got by, with Anna taking in washing and doing other domestic work. In June 1839 Rosetta, their first child, was born. A little over a year later, in October, Anna bore Lewis.

The Douglass family joined the Zion Methodist Church, a black congregation, where he became a class leader. He had become disillusioned with white Christianity over the years. Thinking himself a Christian, he was nonetheless troubled by the hypocrisy of professed Christians, like Thomas Auld, owning slaves, exploiting their labor, and denying to them a Christian education. He had come North with a keen sense of the falseness and duplicity in the church, and his experiences in New Bedford did nothing to change his mind. The Methodist church in that town accepted black congregants almost as a duty, segregating them into "colored pews," and not admitting them to full church fellowship. It was a far different religion from that he and "Father" Lawson had shared when he was a boy. He could have little respect for the Christianity he saw all around him, and the sense of calling he had felt under Lawson's influence became almost completely secular in character.

Douglass had heard of William Lloyd Garrison's *Liberator* while in Baltimore, but in New Bedford he had a chance to read it. He later described his discovery of that abolitionist paper as something of a conversion experience. Here was language and logic cast in a vigorous journalism which showed the slave system to be what he knew it was, an unmitigating evil corrupting both masters and slaves and polluting the entire society in which it thrived.

Douglass attended abolitionist meetings when he could. Some remarks that he made about schemes to colonize blacks in Africa were printed in the *Liberator* of 29 March 1839 which brought him to the attention of Garrison's readers. During the next year he regularly attended meetings at the home of John

Baily, and at an August 1841 meeting of the Bristol Anti-Slavery Society he was brought to Garrison's attention.

Three days later, the antislavery convention on Nantucket Island sat in rapt attention as Frederick Douglass stood to tell them the story of his life as a slave and what had brought him to be a fugitive in the eyes of the laws of the United States.

When John Collins asked him to speak for the Massachusetts Anti-Slavery Society it was with the idea that Frederick Douglass could bring the vividness of his own experience to audiences while standing as living proof of the humanity of slaves. With such an exhibit, the message would be inescapable: the enormity of a system which would deprive such a man of his liberty, denying to him the means and the right of self-improvement. From Collins's point of view, Douglass need merely be physically present and recite his story, but he would not for long be content with such a role.

Quite soon Douglass began to depart from recitations about his personal life and enlarge on broader issues. In 1841 he joined William Lloyd Garrison, Parker Pillsbury, Stephen Foster, and Abby Kelly in a campaign in Rhode Island to defeat a constitution that would extend the franchise to white men without property while explicitly denying the vote to blacks. Traveling in western Massachusetts in the winter of 1841 Douglass began to attack not only slavery in the South but racial prejudice in the North. By 1842, canvassing eastern and central Massachusetts, he seemed to be developing the fullness of his rhetorical style. He had learned well the lessons of *The Columbian Orator*. He was quickly acclaimed not only a powerful speaker but a master of subtleties of the art. Those who heard him were astounded at the sharpness of his mind, his poise and ease on the platform, noting especially his deftness at humor, mimicry, and sarcasm.

Through the fall of 1842 Douglass toured western New York with John Collins and Abby Kelly. In the next year, the American Anti-Slavery Society organized a tour of the western states. They called it the tour of one hundred conventions, and it was to last for six months.

Abolitionists constituted a very small minority of Northern whites. Their views and their speakers were met with hostility even in New England; and in states like Ohio, Indiana, and Illinois hostility and violent language sometimes erupted into mob violence. Douglass, when he was on the platform, was generally a special object of derision. His speeches were normally interrupted by heckling and catcalls. It is a testimony to the power of the oratory of Douglass and his friends that generally hostile audiences were compelled to listen; sometimes they were converted. It was not always the case, however. At the least they were always heckled by some. Often, they were pelted with rotten eggs and vegetables. Sometimes the speakers were lucky to get away with their lives. On 15 September 1843 Douglass was severely beaten by a mob in Pendleton, Indiana, managing to escape with only his hand broken.

Being a fugitive, Douglass was *the* authority on slavery. Others could theorize, but he spoke as a living witness. His message amplified the core of the antislavery argument. In one way or another he would make the points again and again. Slaves shared with other men and women a common humanity. It was an offense to God to hold his human creatures as property, to be bought and sold as animals. It was hypocrisy for the American nation—based as it was on theories of the natural rights of man—to deny life, liberty, and hope for happiness to men and women because they had been stolen from Africa. Slavery was corrupting to all involved in it; slaveowners because it obliged them to be un-Christian, slaves because it brutalized them. It corrupted institutions: governments that indulged and protected it, organized religion and its clergy that strained Christian doctrine to rationalize it. Slave labor was inefficient, impoverishing the many to enrich the few. The slaveowners, despite claims to the contrary, cared little for their slave property. Slaves were meagerly housed, fed, and clothed. Lacking other incentive, they were constantly subjected to the lash. They were denied all possibilities of education and self-improvement, even being barred from firsthand acquaintance with the Bible.

Abolitionists, and certainly Garrison and his followers, had for a decade been denouncing as despotism the slave society, including so-called free states which supported the institution by silence and indifference. Frederick Douglass has experienced in his own life all the claims the abolitionists could make, and he could find there ample illustrations which gave reality and substance to their accusations.

Still, Douglass was a fugitive. His public role placed him in constant danger of being retaken. There were many details of his life he would not tell, fearful of identifying himself as the property of Thomas Auld of St. Michaels, Maryland. So, in all of his public appearances, he held back names and dates and places which might give a bounty hunter a chance to turn him in for cash.

In time the audiences began to demand the specifics he dared not give. Some expressed doubts that he had ever been a slave. He was too effective, too witty, too polished, too eloquent a speaker to have been what he claimed: a self-educated fugitive just four years out of slavery. Douglass, tiring of his expected role, became more and more expansive as he gained public-speaking experience. He began to talk about the fundamental issues: the character of the Constitution, the hypocrisy of Christian churches and their ministers. Such topics were thought beyond the powers of the slave mentality. All of this served those who would cast doubt on his story, damaging his effectiveness on the abolitionists' platform.

Douglass's friends urged him to keep it simple: "Just tell your story." Stephen Foster advised him to speak more haltingly, and John Collins thought it "better to have a little plantation speech." But Douglass refused. He had not broken free of the plantation merely to play the role of an abolistionist's puppet.

One answer was to tell it all, to publish the story of his life, giving the names, places, and dates that he had always held back. That, of course, would be tantamount to giving himself up to Thomas Auld. Some of his friends argued against it, but in the winter of 1844–1845 he sat down to write the narrative of his life. Its publication would be another step in the fugitive's path to freedom.

II

# Apostle of Freedom

*The Narrative of the Life of Frederick Douglass, an American Slave,* published in 1845, was the first of three autobiographies. Revealing details of his life as a slave—the place of his enslavement, his original name, and the name of his master—took a special courage because it placed his freedom in immediate jeopardy. But he refused to discuss his actual means of escape or name the friends who assisted him, for such information would add to the knowledge of slaveowners and their agents, making other escapes more hazardous.

More than an autobiography, the *Narrative,* like Douglass's oratory, was abolitionist polemic, contradicting the premises of the proslavery argument on every page. Slavery, rather than being a means of civilizing and Christianizing backward and pagan Africans, was shown to keep slaves unschooled and unlettered and ignorant of Christianity, except as it might serve the master and the institution. Slaveowners, rather than being gentle, Christian folk, were coarse men and women who dared not follow truly Christian teachings or their own humane and civilizing instincts.

Douglass hardly mentioned his grandmother or his half sisters and brother in this first autobiography. Ten years later, in *My Bondage and My Freedom,* he wrote about them at some length. But in the *Narrative,* he chose to emphasize how slavery undermined family feeling among slaves. It could not be otherwise when a system profited from the natural increase of its subjects, not their moral and circumspect behavior. Slavery also gave men absolute power over their female subjects; one could hardly miss the devastating implications for family life.

The point was clear. It was not a matter of good or bad men treating their subjects well or badly. It was not something one could reform simply with good will. The central evil was the ownership of human beings and the lack of freedom this imposed. That single enormity brought with it inevitable and ugly consequences. Good men and women were no better able to avoid doing evil as slaveowners than could their slave men and women become responsible, productive human beings while in chains. To be an obedient slave meant to be something less than a man, and to be a good master meant to be a benevolent despot, but a tyrant nonetheless.

Real freedom—self-reliant, self-respecting, humanity dignifying freedom—was at bottom the issue, and there could be no substitute for it. Even the kindest, most gentlemanly masters denied this one essential. William Freeland was such a man, and Douglass praised him for being a Christian within the limits of the slave system. He was "the best master I ever had, *till I became my own master.*"

Freedom, too, was a matter of working for one's well-being and not having one's labor expropriated for the profit of others. Douglass became a more productive worker as he became more independent. When Hugh Auld allowed him a degree of freedom as a worker, his earnings greatly increased. He became even more productive in New Bedford, although a fugitive and unable to follow his trade. Freedom allowed him to be a self-reliant person, fully responsible for himself and his family. As for the slaveholders themselves, Douglass confirmed the suspicions of his Northern readers; slave labor spoiled the master class for efficient and productive labor in their own behalf. Slavery made work itself unrespectable.

There would be more than two dozen slave autobiographies published in the nineteenth century, but Douglass's *Narrative* would be the most widely read and the most influential. His celebrity as an abolitionist speaker helped, but it was also because the book was authentic and authoritative, and it was written in a style which managed to expose the ugliness and brutality of slavery without falling into bathos. While it showed how systematic oppression could diminish the quality of human life, it exemplified in the life of the narrator an irreducible human nature and an indomitable human spirit. The reader was not moved to pity for the slave but to anger at a system that oppressed him.

The slave narrative genre was much like the travel literature so popular with Americans at the time, introducing readers to an emotional and spiritual domain that was alien and unimaginable. It presented a world of experience foreign to the readers' clear sense of what was normal, moral, and civilized. There were no more telling arguments against slavery and for freedom than these personal expositions. In an age that celebrated the triumphant human spirit, autobiography was readily converted into effective political weaponry.

The very success of the *Narrative* placed Douglass's liberty in even greater jeopardy. His friends thought it wise for him to leave the country for a while and go to Great Britain. It was for his own safety, of course, but it was also thought that he could help mobilize British abolitionists to work in the American struggle. The British had abolished slavery in the West Indies in 1837. The men and women who had agitated long and hard for that result might help raise money and redirect their moral outrage at the United States.

The trip forced Douglass to leave Anna and the children. The family had moved from New Bedford to Lynn, Massachusetts in 1842, shortly after the birth of their second son, Frederick Jr. Two years later, Charles was born. So Douglass, in going to England, left Anna with four children, one barely a year old. He expected the income from the American sales of the *Narrative* to take the place of what he would have earned from his lectures. To make ends meet, however, Anna went back to work; and the American Anti-Slavery Society helped out occasionally.

On 16 August 1845 Frederick Douglass set sail for Liverpool aboard the Cunard ship, *Cambria,* accompanied by five other abolitionists: the Hutchinson family (a singing group) and James Buffum. Douglass was denied a first-class cabin and was forced to travel steerage. He, nevertheless, made himself well-known to his fellow passengers, he and his friends circulating his book on the promenade deck.

Several passengers asked the captain to arrange for Douglass to lecture. So on the last evening out, he gave a talk on the quarterdeck to a large audience. Two proslavery men heckled him and attempted to break up the meeting. They were restrained only after the captain knocked one down and threatened to put them both in irons. These incidents were the last reminders, for the twenty-month stay in Europe, of the passion and irrationality of American racism.

Douglass experienced in those months abroad what was common to Afro-Americans traveling outside the United States. For the first time in his life he felt himself accepted by the public as a man, nothing more or less. No longer did he have to wonder whether or not he would be served in restaurants and hotels or whether he would be given first-class seats on trains. He was warmly received not only on the lecture platform but in he homes of many notables in Ireland, Scotland, and England. He could be seen in the company of women as well as men without evoking comment.

All of this was dramatically different from day-to-day life in the United States. For even in New England—thought the most liberal section of the country—he and all other black people were daily subjected to humiliating Jim Crow practices in schools, hotels, restaurants, and public transportation. Indeed, white abolitionists themselves were sometimes deeply ambivalent about race. Douglass might well have reflected that the British could better afford tolerance since blacks there were so few in number. But the contrast was too sharp for such speculation. There was quite a bit of irony in a nation's purporting to be the most enlightened and progressive in the world, yet being more despotic and tyrannical than all the monarchies.

Douglass arrived in Britain when the reform spirit there was at its height. While it had been ten years since the emancipation of slaves in the West Indies, abolitionists were still excited from their victory, and there were few who would now argue the proslavery side. If anything, the British were somewhat self-righteous in their attitude about slavery in the United States. They were also alive with demands for temperance and free trade legislation, resulting in the repeal of the Corn Laws in 1846. The debate over the issue of home rule for Ireland was at its most intense, and all of that British dominion was alive with agitation.

Douglass spent his first five weeks in Dublin promoting antislavery as well as lecturing on temperance and Irish home rule. He met the aging Daniel O'Connell, whose speech on Catholic emanicipation had inspired him when he read it in *The Columbian Orator.* He also met the great Irish temperance reformer, Father Theobald Matthew, to whom he gave the temperance pledge. The meetings with O'Connell and other Irish reform leaders—all warm sympathizers with the cause of the American slave—would have great significance for Douglass in the years to come. Irish migration to the United States would reach its peak in the next decade, and it would be Irish immigrants who would be the greatest competitors with blacks for jobs. As they would press for their own rights, they would be some of the most vociferous opponents of political and economic rights for black Americans. Douglass would have cause to reflect on how quickly the oppressed could take on the role of oppressor.

Leaving Ireland, Douglass visited the industrial centers of England. In Birmingham and Manchester, he took active part in agitation to repeal the Corn Laws. Thrown into the excitement over free trade, Douglass learned much about the liberal economic theories of the Manchester school, which were to define his outlook on social and economic questions throughout his life.

Douglass was thrilled to find himself listened to and applauded for his reasoning and effectiveness as a speaker. True, he was notable because he was a black man who had lived as a slave in the United States; that gave him a special hearing. He was, however, more than a display for the antislavery cause. He was viewed as a shrewd interpreter of American society with trenchant opinions on all subjects of social reform.

There was something liberating for Douglass in taking up the fight for causes not his own. He wrote Garrison early in 1846, "I cannot allow myself to be insensible to the wrongs and sufferings of any part of the great family of man." It was not enough for one man to assert a common humanity with the rest of mankind, one had to act the part. "I am not only an American slave, but a man," he wrote, "and as such, am bound to use my powers for the welfare of the whole human brotherhood." A truly free man made everyone's cause of freedom his own.

At least some of Douglass's American abolitionist friends were uneasy about his growing independence while away from home. Some worried lest he fall under the sway of the London Anti-Slavery Committee, considered hostile to the Garrisonians. Wendell Phillips wrote Douglass alerting him to such dangers. Maria Weston Chapman was less direct. She wrote to Richard D. Webb, the publisher in Dublin who was to issue the British edition of Douglass's narrative. She warned Webb to keep an eye on Douglass since he was a man of small means and she worried that money would lure him away from his American friends. Webb apparently thought the best way to warn Douglass was to read him Mrs. Chapman's letter.

Douglass was offended that so little was thought of his integrity. His reply to Mrs. Chapman was sharp. He wrote that he was loyal to his Garrisonian friends, and had never given any of them reason to expect betrayal, especially not for personal gain. Shocked to learn that Mrs. Chapman thought he needed surveillance, he warned her, "If you wish to drive me from the Anti-Slavery Society, put me under overseership and the work is done." The image was calculated to shake an abolitionist's self-righteousness.

Whether or not Douglass would have a permanent overseer while abroad, his conduct was well observed and reported to members of the movement at home. He was not like other men; he had to be above reproach. Dr. J. B. Estlin, of Bristol, wrote Samuel May, Jr. of the many female admirers Douglass had in Britain. He was not sure exactly what it was in the man —his robust stature, his powerful voice, his serious mien, the hint of the exotic in him—but he was a sensation among English women. Some of them, Estlin feared, went beyond the bounds of "propriety, or delicacy as far as appearances are concerned." Estlin assured May that Douglass was, himself, always "guardedly correct, judicious and decorous," nevertheless he felt that this admiring attention from white women was cause for some concern. Estlin thought it might spoil him for his future role in the United States where the slightest association between a black man and white women was the subject of alarm and censure. Estlin also feared that after being in the company of "women of education," Douglass would "feel a void when he returns to his own family."

Such attention to his behavior must have been disturbingly suggestive of the oversight and unfreedom from which he had always been in flight. As he grew more confident, however, it became more clear to Douglass that he had to be his own man. Here was a source of friction that would ultimately cause a bitter rift with the Garrisonians. American abolitionism was rather strictly sectarian. There was little room especially among the Garrisonians for independence of thought and honest disagreement. For the time he was in Britain, however, there would only be hints of the problems yet to come.

In the summer of 1846 Garrison joined Douglass in England. Garrison hoped, with Douglass's help, to urge the establishment of an English antislavery society more friendly to him than he felt the British and Foreign Anti-Slavery Society to be. Both men seemed pleased to be reunited on the platform. They toured with great effectiveness and were gratified with the result.

The two men threw themselves into a raging controversy about the Free Church of Scotland which had broken with the Established Scottish Church in 1843. They raised money throughout Britain and America and received sizable funds from Southern Presbyterian churches. The Glasgow Emancipation Society challenged the propriety of accepting money from slaveholders and began a vigorous campaign to pressure the Free Church to Send Back the Money.

Officers of the Free Church argued that their deputies in America had merely avoided matters which were none of their concern. They had gone to gain support for the Free Church, not to pronounce upon domestic problems in America. While they recognized the system of slavery to be evil, they would distinguish between the character of the system and the "character of the persons whom circumstances have connected therewith." They saw no moral fault in accepting money from slaveholders, which, they felt, in no way suggested their support of the American domestic institution.

On 29 May 1846 Douglass spoke to an antislavery rally at Glasgow's city hall, denouncing the Free Church's behavior as mere opportunism. He was at the height of his rhetorical form. The American antislavery movement, he said, had worked hard—against a hostile and complacent public—to call slavery by its proper name, sin unmitigated. "Man stealing," woman beating, the expropriation of the labor of others, the denial of normal familial and religious development could hardly be called a nicer name. By accepting the money of slaveholders, the Free Church was conveniently ignoring the sinful source of the gift; they were not being neutral in a domestic issue but were working against the antislavery movement. By this implied fellowship with slaveholders the Free Church gave status and respectability to willful, self-serving sinners whose very lives and behavior represented the antithesis of Christianity.

To separate the evil and sinfulness of the system from the men and women served by it was, for Douglass, the most blatant sophistry: "While they would denounce the theft, they would spare the thief; while they would denounce the dice, they would spare the sharper." Douglass recalled that Christ had said, "By their fruits shall they be known." The Free Church's apologists would distinguish between the fruit and the character of the system. "Oh, the artful dodger!" His sarcasm was biting: "Well may the thief be glad, the robber sing, and the adulterer clap his hands for joy." Adultery and the adulterer—slavery and the slaveholder—are not the same: "We may blame the system . . . but not the persons circumstances have connected therewith."

Douglass had become quite adept at using the fact of his slavery to drive home the human realities of the system. "I verily believe," he told his Glasgow audience, "that, had I been at the South, and had I been a slave, as I have been a slave—and I am a slave still by the laws of the United States—had I been there, and that deputation come into my neighborhood, and my master had sold me on the auction block, and given the produce of my body and soul to them, they would have pocketed it, and brought it to Scotland to build their churches, and pay their ministers."

Even more pernicious than the Free Church's acceptance of money from an evil source was their recognition of slaveholders as fellow Christians. Slavery existed in the United States, Douglass insisted, because it was respectable. The slaveholder was respectable, holding important offices in the government and the church. Men "are sold to build churches, women to support missionaries, and children to send Bibles to the heathen." The main goal of abolitionists in the United States was to make the slaveholder disrespectable. The surest way was to deny them the name of Christian. That Christian churches and their clergy would extend fellowship to slaveholders countered the whole thrust of the American antislavery movement. Like other Garrisonians, Douglass insisted that a Christian could find no neutral ground on slavery.

Adding to the agitation over the Free Church, Douglass and Garrison helped the critics of the church make Send Back the Money a slogan of sarcasm and contempt throughout Scotland and England. In the end, the Free Church kept the money but suffered considerable embarrassment in doing so. From the Americans' point of view, however, the issue brought fresh energy into the antislavery movement in Britain and made the necessary connection between the American institution and British behavior.

The hypocrisy of Christian churches over slavery had been a theme in Douglass's *Narrative.* While in Britain, his criticism grew more pronounced. Partly it was because he felt more free to speak, but mainly it was because he felt the strong urge to expose all American hypocrisy to the British.

This penchant embroiled him in a controversy with American clergymen who were in England to attend a world temperance convention in August 1846. While not delegates to the convention, both Douglass and Garrison were invited to attend. Douglass was asked to speak.

Being a temperance man, his sympathies were certainly with the delegates. He drew upon his experience as a slave and as an American to illustrate how alcohol destroyed the will and how slaveholders used whiskey to dull their slaves' sense of manhood and natural aspiration for liberty. Douglass went further, however. He criticized the American temperance movement for its remarkable failure to address the evils of drink in the slave system and for being inhospitable and even hostile to free Northern blacks in the temperance movement. He cited the experience of Philadelphia blacks who attempted to march in that city for the cause of temperance. They were set upon by an angry mob of whites who broke up their march. For all of their otherwise good intentions, Douglass charged, there were no American temperance crusaders who were willing to support such black men in their efforts at "self-improvement."

Douglass's remarks enraged the Americans there and caused Reverend Samuel Hanson Cox, of Brooklyn, to write an attack in the *New York Evangelist.* Douglass, Cox said, was an extremist, motivated politically and for money to shatter the harmony and single-mindedness of the temperance convention. "He lugged in antislavery or abolition . . ." To Cox it was a "perversion and an abuse" to call together thousands in order to be "conspicuous and devoted for one sole and grand object," but "with obliquity, open an avalanche on them for some imputed evil or monstrosity. . . . I say it is a trick of meanness!"

Cox was indignant that Douglass should hold America and Americans up for scorn before an international audience. White Americans were certainly not accustomed to being addressed by a black man who spokc "as if he had been our schoolmaster, and we his docile and devoted pupils." Douglass could hardly be his own man, Cox reasoned, when "the fact is, the man has been petted, and flattered, and used, and paid by certain abolitionists . . . till he forgets himself." Cox was certain that Douglass was doing his own cause more harm than good. Cox's own reactions might serve as a warning. "I came here his sympathizing friend—I am so no more, as I more know him."

Douglass was quick to respond, printing his letter to Cox and the speech in the *Liberator.* He suggested that the aggravating and intolerable insult to Cox was for "a Negro to stand upon a platform, on terms of perfect equality with a pure white American *gentleman*!" Were Cox a Christian, philanthropist, and abolitionist as he claimed himself to be, he would have been delighted to see a fugitive slave on the platform of a world temperance convention. He seemed rather to feel himself and his country "severely rebuked by my presence there."

He could only suspect these to be Cox's feelings: "It may not be quite true. But if it be true, I sincerely pity the littleness of your soul."

Douglass insisted that his speech had been appropriate and invited his readers to judge for themselves. After all, he represented a people who were kept from moral and social betterment by the barriers of slavery and race prejudice. These evils would keep temperance or any other such reform from being effective among them. Certainly, he thought, a world temperance convention would want to know that.

Douglass denied the charge that he had merely followed the promptings of others. Even if that were so, however, he saw nothing wrong in it: "If the thing be right, I should do it no matter by whom prompted." Cox's point had been condescending, perceiving Douglass as the pawn of others. "I acted on my own responsibility," Douglass wrote. "If blame . . . is to fall anywhere, it should fall on me." He had not been paid as Cox had claimed, but he saw nothing wrong in being paid to speak. No more, surely, than being paid to preach. "I should probably have taken pay as readily as you did," he said pointedly, "but it was not offered, and therefore I got none."

What troubled Douglass most were Cox's pretensions to being a Christian reformer with abolitionist sympathy. "Who ever heard of a true abolitionist speaking of slavery as an 'imputed evil,' or complain of being 'wounded and injured' by an allusion to it—and that, too, because the allusion was in opposition to the infernal system?" Cox's professions to the contrary, his letter made any claims as a reformer "brazen hypocrisy or self-deception."

The episode had been a welcome opportunity for Douglass to bring home the fact that the sin of slavery did not only rest on the heads of slaveholders in the South but also with liberal Northerners, like Cox, who were "artful dodgers" when it came to facing up to the realities of slavery. Douglass's attitude and tone while in Britain would echo the indignation of his letter to Cox. American society, its institutions, and its so-called reformers would be the subject of his withering criticism.

In the summer and fall of 1846 Douglass and Garrison toured Britain, sharing the platform. They worked very well together. On 17 August they spoke at the organizational meeting of the Anti-Slavery League for all England, launching an organization with which Garrison knew he could work.

His principal object accomplished, Garrison sailed for the United States in November. The departure of his friend saddened Douglass. He began to feel the length of time he had been away from his home and family. He had to give serious thought to going back.

English friends had offered to send for Anna and the children. They promised him that he would have a comfortable life if he chose to remain in England. He was a fugitive and had left his country partly out of fear of capture, but he had never intended to go into exile. The offer to help him resettle, while generous, did not appeal to him. In his farewell speech in London, 30 March 1847, he told an audience of over four hundred that he would return to the United States despite the hatred and insult that faced black men there at every turn. He saw his purpose and calling to share the plight of his fellow black Americans. He would "struggle in their ranks for that emancipation which shall yet be achieved by the power of truth and of principle"; that battle was in America, not in England. "I glory in the conflict," he exclaimed, "that I may hereafter exult in the victory. I know that victory is certain."

Still a fugitive, his return to America would be dangerous. Nearly two years had passed since the publication of the *Narrative,* it continued to command wide attention. Douglass's public role in Britain had drawn even more attention to himself. If his master had previously only wanted the return of his property, he would want now even more to have this celebrated fugitive under his control.

Several of Douglass's English friends chose to solve the problem by purchasing his freedom. Anna and Ellen Richardson raised a subscription and negotiated the sale. After Douglass's escape Thomas Auld had given ownership in him to Hugh Auld. It was arranged that £150 (approximately $700) be paid for his freedom. Thus Frederick Douglass, now approaching his thirtieth year, by the grace of Hugh Auld's signature, became a free man in the law of the United States.

The purchase of Douglass's freedom kicked up a small storm of controversy among some abolitionists who saw in the act an inconsistency with professed principles. Since abolitionists denied the right of one man to own property in another, there was nothing one could legitimately sell. In short, the purchase of Douglass implied the legitimacy of ownership in him and, therefore, was a proslavery act. The argument, itself, was not frivolous. Such were the grounds for denying the propriety of compensated emancipation. Was the good of freeing slaves fatally compromised by the expediency of compensating the masters for their loss? The British had compensated slaveholders in the West Indies, and some Northern states had paid slaveowners to free their slaves after the American Revolution. While it was a moot question, given the political atmosphere in the United States in the 1840s, still the principle could raise some heated debate.

Garrison defended the purchase as expedient, reasoning that it was wrong to consider the price paid as a *purchase.* Rather, it was a *ransom.* No one ever denied the right or propriety of paying thieves or kidnappers to gain a person's liberty. Why, he asked, should it be different in this case?

Whatever the principle, it did not trouble Douglass. In a letter to Henry C. Wright, published in the *Liberator* of 28 January 1847 Douglass defended the deal. He had not invited or encouraged the action of his friends, and he saw no reason why he should have discouraged them. There would have been a violation of principle, he wrote, if it had been done "*to make me a slave, instead of a freeman*" or "with a view to compensate the slaveholder for what he and they regarded as rightful property." Those who questioned the purchase were wrong in "confounding the crime of buying men *into slavery,* with the meritorious act of buying men out of slavery." The purchasers did not, as some of the critics claimed, presume to "establish my *natural right* to freedom"; he had that as a condition of his humanity. They merely, by the payment of money, removed social and legal obstacles to the exercise of those natural rights. It was an expediency, Douglass explained, nothing more. Had it been his money, he wrote, "I would have seen Hugh Auld *kicking,* before I would have given it to him." He would rather take his chances as a fugitive, paying money only as a last resort to avoid return to slavery. But he would not censure the judgment of his friends.

Douglass found some humor in the argument over the rightness of his purchase. He told a London audience that he was rather pleased that it was Hugh Auld, rather than Thomas, who got the money. "Hugh is a poor scamp," more in need than his brother. But as to the question of right, he said, "I have as much right to sell Hugh Auld as Hugh Auld had to sell me. If any of you are disposed to make of purchase of him, just say the word." Whatever he had suffered at the hands of Hugh and Thomas Auld, however, he "would not traffic in human flesh at all; so let Hugh Auld pass," he said, "for I will not sell him."

On 4 April 1847 Douglass set sail from Liverpool to Boston aboard the Cunard steamer, *Cambria.* For the first time since landing in Britain, he was forced to confront Jim Crow practices. He was denied cabin accommodations because of his color, and he was obliged to take his meals alone and not mix with the other passengers in the salon. Douglass's friends complained to the company, and he wrote a letter to the London *Times.* He pointed out that during his entire sojourn in Britain he had enjoyed rights and privileges equal with other men until "I turned my face toward America." The Cunard line apologized in the press and vowed such a thing would never happen again. Douglass thought this a victory despite the inconveniences to him. Like the Send Back the Money affair, the incident brought home to the British how they, too, were being corrupted by intercourse with a slave society.

Living abroad, Douglass was forced to confront the anomalous relationship Afro-Americans had to their native land. As slave or free, blacks could hardly be considered citizens of the United States. One could hardly be loyal to a nation that seemed to make one's people an exception to the rest of humanity; and loyalty to the United States meant that one honored slavery. Yet to forswear one's country would be to deny one's birthright. Douglass, like other Afro-Americans, struggled with this dilemma.

The Garrisonians had their own sense of loyalty. They honored the principles of the Declaration of Independence, but thought them fatally compromised in the Constitution. Those provisions that regarded a slave as three-fifths of a man, that obliged the national government to engage in the capture and return of escaped slaves, and that empowered the federal government to put down domestic insurrections made the entire nation complicitous in slavery. Thus, the union that was formed under the Constitution was corrupt and undeserving of allegiance.

Douglass shared these views and was unrestrained in his denunciation of the national union. In his farewell address in London, he emphasized that it was a mistake to think of the United States as divided between slave and free states, where the citizens of the latter were advocates of freedom and hostile to slavery. Northerners were the willing allies of slaveholders, and would "bring down . . . the whole civil, military, and naval power of the nation" to crush efforts of slaves to gain their freedom by force. The Northerner would nevertheless proclaim to the world, "let it be clearly understood that we hate slavery."

In returning to the United States Douglass planned "to unmask her pretensions to republicanism." He had no pride in the nation and did not think it deserving of praise: "No, she is unworthy of the name great or free." She stood upon the backs of three million people. Yet, the United States eagerly denounced European despotisms, calling Englishmen "a community of slaves, bowing before a haughty monarchy."

The people of the United States, he said, were "the boldest in their pretensions to freedom, and loudest in their professions of love of liberty," yet no nation exhibited a code of laws as "cruel, malicious, and infernal," as that of the Americans. "Every page," he proclaimed, "is red with the blood of the American slave."

Such strong language was not uncommon in an age of highly polemical oratory. The white Garrisonians were noted for their rhetorical vigor and audacity. But the matter of white men's citizenship was never in question. There was strong desire for black men to prove themselves "good Americans" rather than open themselves to the charge of disloyalty. It took special audacity, therefore, for Douglass to be forthright in denying loyalty to the United States.

He insisted that it was necessary to go outside the country to generate the kind of opinion that would destroy slavery. American slavery was so giant a crime, "so darkening to the soul, so blinding in its moral influence," so calculated to blast and corrupt normal human principles, "that the people among whom it exists have not the moral power to abolish it." No institution in America, neither the church nor the press, nor political parties could be counted on for reform. Since the United States lacked the conviction to overthrow slavery, he welcomed the aid of England.

Over fifty years later, W. E. B. DuBois was to sum up the Afro-American's dilemma as being a "twoness,—American, a Negro, two souls, two thoughts, two unreconciled strivings." Racism imposed on the Afro-American a duality that would continue to be impossible to reconcile. Racial oppression made one loyal first to one's race, but the dilemma evoked a persistent alienation.

Douglass would discover that the dilemma was much less

troubling in the years before the Civil War. Before the war American government and institutions made themselves incompatible to Afro-American citizenship. That made it easier to be a critic and antagonist than it would be after the Thirteenth, Fourteenth, and Fifteenth Amendments had become part of the Constitution.

Whatever strain Douglass felt with the Garrisonians while he was abroad were minor. The question was natural, however, how well Douglass would fit back into the movement. He had already demonstrated a strong will and the desire to be his own man. He had become celebrated as a great speaker and reformer, not merely as an object on exhibition, but as a man whose brilliance and imagination could reshape issues. He had a gift for making white men and women sense a common humanity with him, and, through him, with the slave. Some of Douglass's American friends no doubt imagined that he would be content to pick up where he had left off: the same man only older, more experienced, and free. That was a vain hope.

Douglass had told his English friends that he would like to start a newspaper on his return to the United States. While he had some concern about his ability as a writer, he felt his strong talents were in publicity and that a successful paper, edited by a black man and former slave, would do more to counter prejudice and help the cause than anything else he might do. He was encouraged by English friends who promised to give more than two thousand dollars to the venture.

When he told his American friends about his plans, he got a chilling response. Both William Lloyd Garrison and Wendell Phillips advised against it, and in the strongest terms. Running a newspaper was very difficult for even the most experienced and well-financed editor. At best it was risky, almost destined to failure which could undo much that he had accomplished in building his reputation and poorly reflect on the whole race, giving support to those who insisted that blacks were incompetent. Finally, there were already enough abolitionist papers sharing a small readership. That fact alone could almost doom his paper from the start.

There was something to be said for the argument. There had been several efforts to establish a black newspaper, with no really lasting success. The most notable had been *Freedom's Journal,* which suspended publication in 1827. Ten years later, Reverend Samuel Cornish started the *Weekly Advocate* in New York City. That paper changed its name to the *Colored American,* but folded in 1841. For much of the same time, David Ruggles had published the *Mirror of Liberty* from New York. For less than a year, in 1842, Samuel Meyers, of Albany, New York, published the *Elevator.* William G. Allen, of Troy, New York, did better by five years with the *Clarion,* which stopped publication in 1847. In 1843 the Reverend Henry Highland Garnet edited the short-lived *People's Press,* and in the same year Martin R. Delany tried his hand with the *Mystery* out of Pittsburgh. For eighteen months, ending in June 1848, William Hodge of New York published the *Ram's Horn.* Starting a black newspaper was certainly not an original idea with Douglass, and the history of these efforts were not encouraging.

Even the *Liberator,* after all, was never on secure financial footing. Garrison, his friends, and the American Anti-Slavery Society were often called upon to keep the paper afloat. At its height, it had a circulation of three thousand, of which two-thirds of its readers were black. Garrison and Phillips had reason on their side.

While their argument seemed solely in Douglass's interest, Garrison may also have wanted to avoid having another anti-slavery paper competing with the *Liberator.* Already there was the *Anti-Slavery Standard.* A paper by Douglass with his celebrity, however, might be more than the traffic would bear. Since the *Liberator's* readership was heavily black, it might well be undercut by a successful black paper appealing to a readership unable to support two papers.

On the other hand, Douglass had strong reason to assert himself as a black voice and as a black leader rather than as a principal spokesman for the Garrisonians. Blacks in the North had, in the 1840s, begun organizing and agitating for reform. Douglass himself had participated in one of the first national conventions of colored citizens, held in Buffalo in 1843. Issues pertaining to blacks were paramount. The civil rights of blacks in Northern states, for instance, the question of employment, education, and social improvement of the free black population were lively topics. Black men were raising questions about whether or not to foster black community action, at the risk of strengthening segregation, and whether or not it was in the interest of Afro-Americans to emigrate from the United States. While white reformers had opinions about these questions, it was black consensus that counted. A black man with pretensions of leadership would only weaken his position by being a mere spokesman for one of the several white abolitionist camps.

If Douglass wanted to be a leader among black people, the newspaper was a good idea. Not only could Douglass be his own man but, because of his influence with white abolitionists, he might be able to broaden their outlook to include questions of race relations in America beyond the single issue of slavery.

For the moment, however, Douglass was persuaded to abandon his plans. Aside from the strong opposition of Garrison and his desire not to alienate his friends, there was the fact that there were four black journals extant: the *Ram's Horn,* the *National Watchman,* the *People's Press,* and the *Mystery.* Since he and Garrison were to make a speaking tour of the West, Douglass had enough to occupy him for the moment.

The two men began what was to be a fateful tour in early August 1847. They encountered extremes of triumph and rude hostility. Douglass was lionized in a meeting organized by Philadelphia blacks. In Harrisburg, however, the audience was hostile and violent. As if Douglass needed a reminder that he was not in England, hardly a public place was willing to serve him, and since Garrison refused to eat where his companion could not, the two scarcely had a decent meal.

They were in considerable demand, and their speaking schedule reflected this. They attended five enthusiastic meetings in two days in Pittsburgh. In the Western Reserve of Ohio, there was strong antislavery sentiment. The men spoke before four thousand in New Lyme, moving on to Oberlin. Following Oberlin, the speakers went to Medina, Massilon, Lessburg, and Salem, where they were greeted by crowds of up to five thousand at each location. The tour was exhausting. Most meetings were in the open air. Their voices and health suffered. Douglass was forced to cancel some appearances because of recurring inflammation of his tonsils.

In Cleveland, Garrison collapsed and was unable to continue. Douglass wanted to stay behind until they could continue together. Other engagements waited, however, and Garrison insisted that Douglass go on without him, promising to follow as soon as he was able.

Douglass went on to Buffalo. A week later, he learned that Garrison's condition was critical, and he began to reproach himself for having left his friend. He went on, nevertheless, attending meetings in Rochester and Syracuse. On 8 October Samuel J. May wrote Garrison that Douglass was deeply troubled on arriving at May's home and finding Garrison was not there: "His countenance fell, and his heart failed him."

Garrison was unimpressed by reports of Douglass's solicitude. His recent friend had "not written a single line to me, or to anyone else in this place, inquiring after my health." If that were not enough to cause him annoyance, Douglass resolved late in September that his original idea to start a newspaper was a good one. That decision had a chilling effect on their friendship.

In explaining his final resolve, Douglass wrote an English friend that it had been the western trip itself, his rude reintroduction to the bitterness and ugliness of racial prejudice that convinced him. More than ever, he felt that a journal, well managed and edited by a black man, would be the best weapon against slavery and racial prejudice. He had not brought the matter up to Garrison on the trip, and Garrison thought that inconsiderate and ungrateful. "Such conduct grieves me to my heart," Garrison wrote his wife. "His conduct about the paper has been impulsive, inconsiderate, and inconsistent with his decision in Boston."

Having decided to start his own newspaper, Douglass had to find a location. He thought it would be good to move away from the *Liberator* for reasons of circulation as well as for concerns about continued friction with Garrison. Douglass chose Rochester, New York. He had been led to believe he would be welcome there. The region—the "burnt-over district" of upstate New York extending through the Western Reserve—had been much affected by reform and revival movements. Also there was strong antislavery sentiment in the area. While the abolitionists of the region were more influenced by Theodore Dwight Weld, Arthur and Lewis Tappan, and Gerrit Smith than by William Lloyd Garrison, they were also less doctrinaire and more likely to be tolerant of Douglass's views.

He had been promised help from his English friends, and $2,174 was made available to him. On 1 November 1847 Douglass moved his family to Rochester, and prepared for his new career. On the same date, the *Ram's Horn* announced the inception of a new publication, the *North Star,* to be published and edited by Frederick Douglass. "The object of *The North Star* will be to attack slavery in all its forms and aspects; advocate Universal Emancipation . . . promote the moral and intellectual improvement of the colored people; and to hasten the day of freedom to our three million enslaved fellow-countrymen."

Douglass declared a new independence. "I shall be under no party or society, but shall advocate the slave's cause in the way which in my judgment, will be best suited to the advancement of the cause."

This new declaration of independence, like his escape from slavery, was Douglass's claim to manhood and personal freedom. In this instance it was freedom from a role imposed and defined by those who called themselves his friends and yet considered his independence to be ingratitude. Doubtless, Thomas and Hugh Auld had considered him an ingrate for escaping from privileged and benign treatment as a slave. Having been given an inch, he took "the ell," as Hugh Auld had put it. But if Douglass imagined he could leave the Garrisonians and go in peace, he was mistaken. His erstwhile friends were no less possessive than the Aulds. They did not own him and could not be paid off, but their bitterness would rankle even so.

# III
# Self-reliance

DOUGLASS'S New England friends should have understood his break for independence. In accord with the Emersonian dogma of self-reliance, they certainly would have approved the principle behind it. The genius, the spark of the divine, the spirit in every man must be allowed to realize itself. Too slavish an obedience to duty, conformity to society's demands, or loyalty to faction or party merely stifled the inner spirit which was the essence of the true self. Having faith in oneself—one's instincts, one's intuition—was the only way to break free to one's divine calling. Abolitionists, like Garrison, understood this well; the fundamental evil of slavery was that it placed this spirit in chains.

Douglass was a believer in that faith, his own experience exemplifying that indwelling spark in the lowliest, in the slave. It was easier, however, to believe than to act on such principles. The Garrisonians never quite understood that the loyalty they required, the doctrinal conformity they demanded of their friends, would stifle the very spirit they would liberate. And Douglass would find in race itself a "faction" or "party" which neither white men nor black men could ignore or transcend.

The independent path was, despite its pitfalls and futility, the only way for a man who wanted to be free. It did not take Douglass long to learn, however, that a well-edited newspaper was not exactly eagerly awaited by the world. On 3 December 1847 he began publication of his weekly, the *North Star.*

Thanks to his English friends, be began free of debt, but in less than six months Douglass was forced to mortgage his home to keep the paper going.

His original plan was to devote the major part of his own time to the newspaper, curtailing his activities on the lecture platform. He brought in Martin R. Delany, who had published the *Mystery* out of Pittsburgh, to promote the paper in the countryside, selling subscriptions for two dollars a year. William C. Nell, an avid black Garrisonian, was to be co-publisher. Two white apprentices set type and locked up the pages. As his boys grew older they worked under the printers to learn the trade.

By June 1848 Martin Delany was dropped as coeditor. He had many other interests and he was proving to be of little support. William C. Nell continued with the paper for two years, but Douglass's growing support of political abolitionism and the Liberty party forced him to choose between Douglass's paper and continued loyalty to Garrison's antipolitical stand. Nell chose fidelity to his New England friends, sharing their hostility to Douglass.

An English woman, Julia Griffiths, came to be Douglass's strongest supporter and ally on the paper. He had met her at Newcastle-on-Tyne, and found her deeply committed to the antislavery cause. She came to Rochester in 1848 and immediately pitched in to help with the paper. She moved into the Douglass home, became the business manager of the paper, and quickly put its finances in order.

Douglass came to rely on Julia Griffiths; she was his most loyal and selfless friend during those years. She served him in ways that Anna, who remained illiterate, could not. She helped him with grammar, syntax, and editorial work. While he had become a master of oratory, being self-taught he naturally remained unsure of written style. She gave him the assurance he needed. She guided his continuing education, often reading aloud to him from the classics and the canon of English literature.

Despite all Douglass and Griffiths could do, the paper foundered badly after 1855. She returned to England in the hope of raising enough to keep the paper going. While she had some success, the paper had to be reduced in size and, beginning in 1860, published as a monthly.

Julia Griffiths remained in England, never to return to Rochester. That decision, and probably her return to England in the first place, was influenced by the fact that she had become a target of Douglass's critics. Her closeness with Douglass excited rumors, and her open criticism of the Garrisonians widened the rift between the old comrades. Perhaps she came to see herself as a liability to her friend. Although she never returned, she and Douglass would remain close friends, continuing their correspondence for over forty years.

Early in 1851 Douglass's neighbor, Gerrit Smith, who had been the principal supporter of the ineffective and costly *Liberty Party Paper,* agreed to merge with the *North Star,* Douglass maintaining control but opening the pages to Liberty party news. Smith would give the paper a subsidy. The new, combined publication would be called *Frederick Douglass' Paper.* The agreement between Douglass and Smith merely verified to the Garrisonians the final apostasy of Douglass. After that merger he was called an "enemy."

The merger merely delayed the inevitable. By 1859 he was forced to reduce the size of his weekly, and still its costs exceeded its income. To meet the additional expense of serving his foreign subscribers, he published a concise version called *Douglass' Monthly.* Finally, in 1860, after thirteen years of weekly publication in which he never missed an issue, he announced that he would no longer publish *Frederick Douglass' Paper.* He continued printing the monthly until 1863, when that, too, expired.

While Douglass was saddened by the demise of his paper, he had very little reason for embarrassment. Although never self-supporting, none of the major antislavery papers were. It remained through its life the most important vehicle for black writers and reformers, always well written and well edited. He had seen his journalism, as he saw his life, as necessarily exemplary. The world looked on to praise or blame, and his papers had to be as good as or better than white papers of their kind —and they were.

The publishing enterprise certainly helped liberate Douglass's genius. Through his years with the paper, his mind grew, along with his sense of power and authority. Years later he would say, reflecting on his long life, that if he wrote or said anything of any importance, it was between the years 1848 and 1860. During those years he came into his own.

The true doctrine of self-reliance cautioned against any mean egotism which would seek mere self-aggrandizement and self-interest. Since the essential inner genius corresponded to the soul of every man, self-reliance would lead one to universal principles and ideals. To be merely a black man serving the interests of black people would be petty and unworthy, but what Douglass found compelling in this cause was that it so perfectly exemplified the general corruption of the American people and society. There was a broad front of needed reform, with abolition and racial justice at the center. Douglass would support them all, principle foremost, in order to avoid being thought narrow and self-seeking.

In Rochester, Douglass remained a temperance man, still rebuking the American temperance leadership for not welcoming blacks as members. His papers made an appeal for the distribution of free land to the people, challenging the government's policy of giving "millions upon millions of acres of public lands to aid soulless railroad corporations to get rich." He editorialized against the growing tendencies toward monopoly, supported the peace movement of Elihu Burritt, urged reform in the treatment of seamen whose lot at sea was hardly better than that of slaves, and joined in efforts to abolish capital punishment in New York State.

The cause to which he devoted the most energy, next to

abolition and racial justice, was that of women's rights. It was reasonable enough that he did so. Women's plight, because they lacked most of the political and economic rights of white men, was in ways equivalent to that of blacks. Women were strong allies in the abolition movement. Douglass found among the antislavery women the hardest workers and his most willing supporters. Some were effective speakers like Abby Kelly, and Lydia Maria Child was the very able editor of the *Anti-Slavery Standard.* It was little wonder that the *North Star* should carry the slogan Right Is of No Sex.

The meeting at Seneca Falls, New York on 19 and 20 July 1848, which launched the movement for women's rights, was announced in the *North Star.* Douglass was among the sixty-seven who attended. He supported fully the Declaration of Sentiment and the list of demands: the right of women to personal and religious freedom, the right to a hearing as witnesses in court, the right to equality in marriage, the right to their own children, the right to hold property in their own names, the right to claim their own wages, and the right to education and equality in trades and professions. They also demanded the right to vote and hold public office.

These last items caused the only major controversy. Many felt that the demand for the vote would be seen by the public —by women as well as by men—as so outrageous as to bring ridicule on the work of the convention. Even without raising the suffrage issue, they were called "hermaphrodites" and "Aunt Nancy men"; with it, they risked being dismissed as hare-brained by the general public.

Elizabeth Cady Stanton insisted that the demand for the vote be adopted. Looking for support in the convention, she turned to Frederick Douglass. "I knew Frederick, from personal experience, was just the man for the job." She was not wrong. Douglass seconded her motion and gave a strong speech in its support, arguing that political equality was essential to women's liberation.

Douglass continued at the forefront of the movement. Hardly a women's rights meeting occurred in the 1850s without him as one of the principal speakers. It was partly due to his influence that the first National Woman's Rights Convention of 1850 adopted the slogan Equality Before the Law Without Distinciton of Sex or Color. In many ways, Douglass made the rights of blacks and the rights of women one. When Gerrit Smith asked Susan B. Anthony how best he might be kept informed of what the women's movement was doing, she told him simply to read Douglass's paper.

Toward the end of his life, looking back on what he had done, he found his work in the women's rights movement especially gratifying. "When I ran away from slavery, it was for myself," he said; "when I advocated emancipation, it was for my people; but when I stood up for the rights of women, self was out of the question, and I found a little nobility in the act."

Being independent was all well and good, but the facts of life forced Douglass to see himself as one with all black Americans; his fate tied to theirs. Self-reliance for blacks would be qualified by the burden of race. One could never be an individual in that ideal sense as long as one was bound to the reputation of race. Though white American idealists and reformers could indulge the notion of an independent, private integrity, Douglass could not. His move to Rochester merely strengthened his sense of himself as a national spokesman for blacks, free and slave, Northern and Southern.

It had become increasingly obvious since his first days in the North that the issue was not simply between freedom and slavery. Free blacks were seldom served in hotels or restaurants. They were segregated in trains and coaches and denied free access to education. Professional and apprenticeship training was not open to them, and thus they were relegated to the most menial occupations. Even so-called Negro work, such as that of longshoremen, draymen, waiters and barbers, would be threatened in the 1840s and 1850s when European immigrants were given preference over black men in employment.

Hardly a Northern state admitted blacks to full citizenship. The western states of Ohio, Indiana, Illinois, and Michigan not only denied blacks the right to vote, but had statutes restricting their right to settle and own property. Pennsylvania and Connecticut denied blacks the vote outright, and New York imposed on them a special property qualification. In Massachusetts, the most liberal of the Northern states, blacks were segregated in the public schools. Cultural resources like museums, lyceums, and theaters were generally closed to them. Black reformers, including Douglass, were constantly insulted, harrassed, and often threatened with violence.

Blacks could hardly rely on white reformers and their organizations to advocate their cause. In their own right they hoped to shape a national platform from which to appeal to the public, protest indignities and encourage and direct their fellows. Frederick Douglass joined with other Northern blacks in a series of national conventions between 1840 and 1855. These conventions presented Afro-Americans as a national group whose interests were identical with national ideals. The details of their platform changed over those fifteen years to reflect shifting political realities—especially the growing Southern influence over national policy. Douglass's own attitudes changed—his strategies for reform, his perceptions of reality—reflecting at each turn more the perspective of his fellow blacks than the dictates of Garrisonian dogma.

The first convention Douglass attended was held at Buffalo in 1843. He was then, of course, still solidly within the Garrisonian camp, and he played the loyal role. He led the slight majority which defeated Reverend Henry Highland Garnet's resolution calling for slave insurrections. Echoing his New England mentor, Douglass argued that moral suasion was the only effective way to end slavery.

The convention of 1848 addressed itself mainly to Northern blacks. Douglass was the principal author of its "Address to the Colored People of the United States." He would rouse them from their apathy to join in the fight against slavery. Northern blacks merely deluded themselves in thinking of their fate as separate from slaves. True, they were "not slaves to individuals," Douglass wrote, "not personal slaves, yet in many respects we are slaves of the community." They should be at the forefront of the abolitionist movement. "Every one of us should be ashamed to consider himself free, while his brother is a slave."

The struggle could be advanced, the address continued, by Northern blacks organizing in existing antisalvery societies, establishing others where need be; working with whites where possible, alone where necessary. Race improvement would come through self-improvement, which meant economic independence and self-reliance.

Blacks had to place themselves in occupations which would make whites in the community "as dependent on us as we are on them." By moving into the mechanical trades and farming in large numbers, they would become indispensible to the community. That would be the beginning of the end of racial prejudice and oppression. With an independent and self-reliant Northern black population, slavery in the South could not survive. Despite its frank awareness of the realities of Northern black life, his address was encouraging and optimistic about the future, recommending diligence, aggressive self-development, and purposeful organization.

Events, however, would not support that optimism. By the end of the decade Northern whites had become even more resistant to respecting the political and economic rights of blacks. The Compromise of 1850 seemed to mean capitulation on the part of Northerners to the interests of slaveholders. The Fugitive Slave Act, which was a part of that legislation, in fact placed Northern blacks, fugitive and free, in jeopardy of enslavement. It drove home the oneness of free blacks and slaves, even more clearly than the "Address to the Colored People." When Douglass and his committee wrote the "Claims of Our Common Cause," a report on the convention of 1853, they were no longer so confident of the future.

The 1853 report was addressed to all the American people, voicing the appeal of "American citizens asserting their rights on their native soil." It was their demand for rights as citizens, to the jury box, to "the complete and unrestricted right of suffrage." They asked that blacks be admitted to "open and equal competition" with whites so that they might rise "agreeable to their merits and attainments," and that state and national governments cease efforts to encourage emigration of Afro-Americans from their homeland.

Furthermore, the address asked that the birthright citizenship status of Afro-Americans be honored in the laws of the land. They demanded that "the word *'white'* be struck from the pre-emption act." They asked that the Fugitive Slave Act of 1850 be repealed and that the law of 1793 (obliging the federal government to capture and return fugitive labor) be construed to apply only to "apprentices, and others really owing service or labor; and not slaves, who can *owe* nothing."

The "Claims of Our Common Cause" was a demand that justice be given free blacks, an assertion of citizenship, and a promise that blacks would remain and presevere. In a letter to Gerrit Smith, Douglass wrote of "my address" being "somewhat tame, but perhaps it will reach some minds which a more spirited document would not."

Douglass also tried in the 1853 convention to devise a scheme to advance economic independence for Northern blacks through support for an industrial school.

In March 1853 Harriet Beecher Stowe had asked his advice as to the best thing she could do to help free blacks improve their condition. She was going to England and thought she might be able to raise money for a suitable cause. Douglass met her at her home in Andover and impressed her with the idea of a manual training school which would instruct blacks in useful and productive trades. At her request, he spelled out the full argument in a letter that she planned to use to solicit funds.

Douglass read that letter to the convention, hoping to persuade the meeting to give the project the kind of support it would need. Overcoming objections of those of Garrisonian persuasion who argued such a school would be a black school after all, compromising their principles against segregation, Douglass gained the convention's support. He was made chairman of the Committee on the Industrial School which set out to raise funds sufficient to establish the institution. The school would be open to all, yet everyone knew it would be "complexional in character." Women would be accepted as students and faculty, as the school would set out "to aid in providing for the female sex, methods and means of enjoying an independent and honorable income."

Douglass threw himself into fund raising for the industrial school, but very little money came in. Much of his hope rested on Harriet Beecher Stowe, who had been very enthusiastic about the project when he spoke with her. She had promised to raise money, but for reasons never made clear she changed her mind and nothing much came from her. As for support from the Garrisonians, they objected on the grounds that it would reinforce patterns of racial segregation, and dismissed the leadership as suffering under a *"morbid state of mind."*

The other important work of the 1853 convention was the attempt to establish the National Council for Colored People. Following the pattern of national political parties, the convention leaders hoped to create in the council a permanent national organization with representatives from each of the ten Northern states where there would be grass-roots representation in elected local councils. Douglass threw himself enthusiastically into this work, but like the industrial school, nothing came of it.

By the end of the 1853 convention, Douglass would know the hard fact that effective independence would be as difficult for him to maintain among blacks as among whites. The convention movement was rife with factions, many merely black advocates of white reformist groups. Given their fundamental powerlessness, it was reasonable enough that blacks would readily accept the leadership of whatever white faction was most congenial. Nevertheless, this worked against the consolidated efforts of the convention movement, and it undermined such enterprises as the National Council for Colored People whose first and last meeting in 1854 failed for want of a quorum.

Black Garrisonians, like William C. Nell and Charles L. Remond, had always caused some dissension within the convention movement. Echoing Garrison's assimilationism, they considered the conventions dangerously race conscious and separationist. Sharing Garrison's antipolitical stance, they were also uneasy with the search for expedient tactics within the framework of the Consititution. These differences were never by themselves disruptive. The political events of the 1850s and the growing dispair among some black leaders, however, had the combined effect of shattering the movement.

The Compromise of 1850, with its Fugitive Slave Act, had been bad enough, placing as it did the liberty of Northern blacks in jeopardy. Arguing the case of Afro-American citizenship, as the 1853 convention did, bespeaks their latent anxiety; and they had better reason to worry than they knew. Four years after the convention published "Claims of Our Common Cause," Chief Justice Roger B. Taney wrote for the majority of the Supreme Court in *Dred Scott v. Sanford.* This decision denied that those of African descent whose ancestors "had been imported as slaves" had any claim to American citizenship, whatever their treatment in one or another state. From the nation's beginnings, he argued, blacks "had no rights which the white man was bound to respect."

The convention of 1853 could not have anticipated the Court's complete acceptance of the interests and values of slaveholders as the basis of national law and policy. In declaring the Missouri Compromise unconstitutional (it had been fifty years since *Marbury* v. *Madison,* the only previous time it had taken such an audacious step), the Court denied the national government power to restrict slavery anywhere in the country, insisting that the slaveholder's property be honored and protected everywhere. Following the *Dred Scott* decision, few could believe that the fate of Northern blacks was separate from that of slaves.

Such events of the 1850s caused many blacks to despair of any future in the United States. The call by black leaders for emigration out of the country increased. This clamor represented a fundamental, ideological conflict and threw the 1855 convention in Philadelphia into disarray. That convention would be the last effort by blacks before the Civil War to develop a national organization and platform for reform.

Frederick Douglass, from his first public speech in New Bedford, had always opposed emigration. He joined with the Garrisonians in making the American Colonization Society a primary target of attack. His hostility to such plans, coming from blacks or whites, would be consistent throughout his life. It was not that Douglass doubted that blacks could find a more comfortable and dignified life outside the United States. He had been tempted himself to accept the offer of his English friends to establish him and his family in England. It was, rather, that he believed Afro-Americans should insist upon a recognition of their legitimacy as Americans. More important, he believed that those blacks who would leave the country would be abandoning slaves to their fate, which would be a selfish act. Free blacks were obliged, he felt, to fight in their native country for the emancipation of their fellows in chains. In the 1850s he would find two formidable black leaders who saw matters differently: Reverend Henry Highland Garnet and Martin R. Delany.

Garnet had long been opposed to colonization, but by the late 1840s had come to doubt that blacks could win freedom or gain full citizenship in the United States. He came to believe, however, that the black man's sojourn in America was providential. A selective migration of Afro-Americans to Africa—skilled persons and Christian ministers—could help bring Africa into the modern world, implanting Western institutions and practices. While traveling in England in 1850, he got support for these ideas from the African Aid Society, which had been working for a decade to Christianize and westernize Africans, with the aim of furthering a healthier Anglo-African intercourse. When, in 1855, the African Civilization Society was formed in the United States, Garnet was among its leadership.

There were not many Afro-Americans who were willing to follow Garnet. Those, like Douglass, who had fought so long against the American Colonization Society could not be persuaded that this new organization was any different. The fact that the African Civilization Society was a white enterprise made many suspicious that it was a front for the older organization.

Martin R. Delany, the Pittsburgh physician and one-time Douglass associate, was the foremost emigrationist. He, too, like Garnet, was a late convert, opposing such schemes as late as 1851. By the following year, however, he had published *The Condition, Elevation, Emigration, and Destiny of the Colored People of the United States,* in which he argued that Afro-Americans had little choice but to leave. Anything short of full equality with whites was insulting and impossible. Status made no difference, slave or free, blacks were denied the right to vote; nor had they any rights and privileges except as the white man was willing to grant them. "Where then," he asked free blacks, "is our political superiority to the enslaved?" Emigration was the only way Afro-Americans could gain control over their own lives. As a place to go, he proposed Central or South American or the East Coast of Africa.

By the 1853 convention in Rochester, Delany had already converted to emigration. The convention debated and rejected proposals supportive of such schemes. Perhaps the convention's concentration on the legitimacy of Afro-American citizenship was as much for blacks like Delany as for whites who denied it.

Delany called a convention of black sympathizers to be held in Cleveland in 1854, which published its position in *The Political Destiny of the Colored Race on the American Continent.* The convention established a commission to report on the feasibility of blacks migrating to various locations. By the end of the decade Delany had explored the Niger River Valley, made treaties with certain Yoruba chiefs which would permit limited Afro-American settlement, and returned to the United States to promote his plan. Nothing came of it. Aside from continued hostility to the idea among black Americans, wars among the Yorubas nullified Delany's treaties, and the onset of the Civil War changed things. For if it would be, as some claimed, a war to resolve finally the question of slavery and freedom in the United States, then even men like Delany would have to see greater possibilities for the Afro-American to achieve true equality.

The upsurge of emigrationist sentiment never gained popular support among blacks in the years before the war. It succeeded in the 1850s, however, in dividing black leadership at just the time when national organization among them had seemed possible.

Frederick Douglass's opposition to emigration was constant. He considered it the most pernicious idea among Afro-American spokesmen. Emigration would deny the black man's birthright, in conceding to, in fact if not in word, the white American contention that blacks had no claim to citizenship. It was the black man's duty to remain in America, force the United States to live up to its ideals and its divine destiny to be a Nation of Nations. Emigration schemes, especially those designed by Delany and Garnet, would draw off only the most enterprising and skilled black Americans, the very ones, as Douglass saw it, who were needed most in the struggle in America. And, to him, the most telling criticism was that the emigrant would be abandoning slaves to their fate. To Douglass that was unconscionable, both a sign of mean egotism and unabashed self-interest.

This last argument was strong and difficult for black emigrationists to answer. Few of them had been slaves themselves and, as Delany, often seemed more offended about the lowly status of free blacks than the fact that most blacks were held in bondage. The National Emigration Convention urged that one should not hide behind "the plea of our brother bondsmen in ignorance. . . . We are no longer slaves, as were our fathers, but freemen." For Douglass that was ignoble.

The difference between the emigrationists and Douglass was not one of "black nationalism," of those who promoted the idea of a black nation and those who would not. Both sides would use the rhetoric of nation, echoing the general view of the United States as a Nation of Nations. This was surely Douglass's view of America's proper destiny, seeing the Afro-American as one of the many nations which would comprise the American people. Actually, as he saw it, emigration was a denial of black nationhood, for as he wrote Harriet Beecher Stowe, "individuals emigrate, nations never."

Douglass may not have known when he established the *North Star* how far that independent stand would pull him away from William Lloyd Garrison and the other New England abolitionists. The move to Rochester had taken him out of the Garrisonian orbit, and his immersion in the ongoing struggle of Northern blacks forced him to consider many issues differently from the way they were viewed by his erstwhile friends.

At first there was a subtle drifting away, marked by changes in perspective. On questions having to do with violence, for instance, it became increasingly difficult for him to express convictions plausible to most blacks yet consistent with Garrison.

Garrison had been strongly influenced toward pacifism by both Benjamin Lundy, the Quaker abolitionist and editor of

*Genius of Universal Emancipation,* and John Humphrey Noyes, the perfectionist and utopian leader. Garrison's abolitionism, as all his reform precepts, assumed the perfectability of the human being when guided by his innermost moral spirit. Divinity was indwelling but could not thrive in an atmosphere of moral compromise, even to achieve just ends. Garrison, therefore, could not countenance violence as a means to end slavery. Rather, one must expose the evil of slavery, in the most clear and uncompromising terms, so that the consciences of men and women would be awakened to the corruption of which they were a part. Since violence was itself an evil, it would not only compromise the reform enterprise, but corrupt it as well. Thus, *nonresistance* and *moral suasion* were central precepts of Garrisonian dogma. They were the means by which Americans could be brought to see their shame and be moved to reform.

Such an argument had very little to say to the slave, or to anyone oppressed. For the shame of a victim is of a different order than that of the victimizer. Blacks, indeed, were most likely to feel that their shame was in their nonresistance. They were convinced that docility and stoical acceptance of one's lot was, whatever its moral strength, held in contempt by the general public. There was the sense that one must win one's place and one's dignity in the eyes of other men, and that had to be done by force. The rhetoric of free blacks was filled with directions to do the *manly* thing. Should a slave not use violence against his master? Should free blacks and fugitives not use violence to protect themselves from slave hunters and kidnappers? The Garrisonians were ambivalent about these questions; Douglass, as a black spokesman, could not be.

As a slave, Douglass never had qualms about violence, he merely lacked the means. He fought Covey and the Baltimore shipyard workers, as recalled in his *Narrative,* with no apologies. Yet, he had become enough a Garrisonian to preach moral suasion against Henry Highland Garnet's call for slave uprisings at the 1843 Buffalo convention. It could not, even then, have been a deep conviction because in his London farewell address he allowed his fancy full rein: welcoming an American war with a foreign power for at the "first trumpet call to freedom—millions of slaves are ready to rise and to strike for their own liberty." The events of the 1850s—the Fugitive Slave Act, the *Dred Scott* decision, "Bleeding Kansas" —would remove any ambiguity he might still have had.

Nonviolence and moral suasion were certainly unrealistic positions for fugitive slaves or those who would help them toward freedom. Violence, after all, was implicit in the act of escaping, and civil disobedience was incumbent on those who would shield them or help them along their way. From the 1830s fugitives, like Douglass himself, had made their way to the North, some going on to Canada. If the number of fugitives did not increase after 1850, it seemed so because the new Fugitive Slave Law emboldened masters and their agents to search out their slaves in the North; this often resulted in open and violent confrontations between defiant whites and blacks. Douglass wholeheartedly supported such direct action, making his Rochester home a major way station for fugitives on their way to Canada. If such action led to bloodshed, Douglass was not much troubled.

In 1851 Edward Gorsuch, his son, nephew, and a United States marshal came into Christiana, in Lancaster County, Pennsylvania, with warrants to capture and return four fugitives to Maryland. Led by William Parker, a large number of local blacks and whites resisted. A pitched battle resulted in which Gorsuch was killed and his son critically wounded. Parker and his brother-in-law, fearful of apprehension for murder, fled to Canada. Frederick Douglass helped them cross the border. In other instances he made it clear that he had no qualms about violence or killing in the cause of freedom. Reacting to the death of James Batchelder, a deputy charged with holding back the would-be rescuers of Anthony Burns, Douglass editorialized on 2 June 1854 that the man had "forfeited his right to live . . . his death was necessary as a warning to others." This was a far cry from moral suasion.

When he first met John Brown, in late 1847, Douglass had been open to any plan for freeing slaves, even those involving violence. Brown had put before him a scheme to bring the downfall of slavery, and Douglass had found "much to commend it." Yet, speaking to a New York audience in October 1847, it was Garrisonian language that Douglass used. Slavery he said, "has fastened its roots deep into the heart of the nation, and nothing but God's truth and love can cleanse the land. We must change the moral sentiment." In the ensuing ten years, however, Douglass became a confidant of Brown, accepting the old man's view that slavery was a state of war.

Frederick Douglass may not have been aware when he met John Brown how deadly serious the old man was or how, for him, the "state of war" was more than mere rhetoric and his plans of violent confrontation with the "slave power" more than fanciful dreams. In time, Douglass was to listen to the old man and be strongly influenced by him. So, in addition to the events of the 1850s, pushing Douglass to accept violence as inevitable and necessary, John Brown was to make himself much more a part of Douglass's life, ultimately attempting to enlist him in his scheme.

Originally, as Douglass understood it, Brown was planning to establish a chain of hide-outs in the mountains running from Virginia and Maryland into the Northern states. By a series of raids on plantations and farms, slaves would be liberated and guided through these mountain redoubts into the North and Canada. The heartiest of the slaves would be recruited to strengthen the guerrilla bands and extend the operation. Despite some reservations, Douglass was attracted to the idea.

It may have been the ten years spent brooding over his plan, or it may have been the bloody fights with proslavery forces in

Kansas, but by 1858 Brown was contemplating something much more audacious and yet more futile.

On 20 August 1859 he met with Douglass and a fugitive, Shields Green, who had been staying in Douglass's home. They met in a stone quarry near Chambersburg, Pennsylvania. For the first time, Douglass learned that instead of the original plan, Brown intended to raid a government arsenal at Harper's Ferry, Virginia, hold leading citizens as hostages while slaves in the surrounding area were rounded up. Brown had also contemplated the establishment of a free state in the mountains and had drafted a constitution with that in mind.

Douglass was shocked. Attacking a government installation guaranteed reprisals by federal troops and certain failure. Besides, there was no way out for either the raiders or the slaves. The original plan made sense; this one was suicidal. Brown was unmoved by Douglass's criticism. His new plan, he thought, would dramatize the evils of slavery and bring the seriousness of it—the deadliness of it—to the nation's attention. He was unable to persuade Douglass. Shields Green chose to "go with the old man," becoming the only slave to be a part of Brown's army of blacks and whites.

On October 17 while lecturing in Philadelphia Douglass heard the news of John Brown's capture following his raid on Harper's Ferry. Like several white abolitionists with whom Brown had conferred, Douglass had good reason to fear that he might be charged as an accomplice in Brown's conspiracy. Indeed, the *New York Herald* carried exaggerated accounts of Brown's confessions which, according to that Democratic paper, implicated Gerrit Smith, Frederick Douglass, and *"Other Abolitionists and Republicans."*

On the advice of friends, Douglass crossed the border into Canada, outside the reach of American courts. Whatever the truth of his involvement with Brown, he knew better than to place his fate in the hands of American justice especially in the hysterical atmosphere following the raid.

Douglass had been planning for some time a return to England. So he stayed in Canada until his departure on November 12 from Quebec. He remained in Britain until May 1860, returning home on the news of the death of his youngest child, Annie.

In June 1860 Frederick Douglass wrote James Redpath of his regrets at not attending a memorial for John Brown. "I have little hope," he wrote, "of the freedom of the slave by peaceful means." The slaveholders, he said, "were well beyond the reach of moral and humane considerations."

In the early 1840s abolitionists were forced to consider whether or not the Constitution, as written when the Union was formed, accepted slavery as part of the commonwealth, protecting it under the law. Southerners and proslavery advocates argued that the organic or fundamental law under which the states came into the Union was in no way hostile to slavery, but protected the institution and citizens' rights to own slaves as property. If one accepted this view, there was no remedy for slavery within the framework of the Constitution, or in the political system it established.

On this position William Lloyd Garrison, his followers, and slaveholders were in accord. As Garrison saw it, the Constitution created a Union which would accommodate slaveholders and their human property. While slavery was nowhere mentioned in the document, it defined as three-fifths of a person those who were not free and not Indians; it protected the importation of slaves until 1808; it provided a legal basis for federal legislation aiding in the return of fugitive slaves; and it obliged the Union to protect slave states from domestic insurrection. By recognizing and protecting slavery, the Constitution violated both human rights and Christian principles, as Garrison saw it. It could not, therefore, be relied on as law, nor could the Union it formed command the allegiance of moral men and women. For Garrison, one's obedience was to "higher law." Man-made constitutions must "harmonize with the law of God or be set at naught by upright men."

In the spring 1843 meeting of the Massachusetts society, Garrison proposed a resolution that "the compact that exists between North and South is 'a covenant with death and an agreement with Hell'—involving both parties in atrocious criminality—and should be immediately annulled." This resolution passed by a wide margin, and the *Liberator* began to carry the motto No Union with Slaveholders! From 1842, week after week, Garrison was to appeal in the *Liberator* for a peaceful separation of the North and the South. With such a constitution, disunion was the only effective way to free oneself of the evil it engendered. Thus, Garrison took up the leadership of that faction of abolitionists which would dissolve the union under the Constitution to reestablish a union of free states. This new, organic law would conform to human rights as articulated in the Declaration of Independence and in their version of Christian principles.

For this faction efforts to bring about reform within the political system were not only perverse but pernicious, compromising moral principles for questionable gain. This position heightened the differences between Garrison and his old enemies in the antislavery movement, Lewis and Arthur Tappan, but it also drew the line between him and those, like Gerrit Smith, James G. Birney, Henry B. Stanton, and Joshua Leavitt, who sought effective reform through political action in the Liberty party.

After Douglass's move to Rochester, his faith in Garrisonian doctrine was in jeopardy. Open to the influence of Gerrit Smith, he would hear the case for political action free of the contempt the New Englanders placed on it. In his new role, bidding for leadership among blacks, Douglass would find the moral self-righteousness of disunion unsatisfactory. If the North and South were to separate, slavery would continue in the South and racism would remain untouched. Only the consciences of men like Garrison would be assuaged.

As Douglass continued to wrestle with the question of the nature of the Constitution and the moral propriety of political action, he began to change his mind. He wrote Gerrit Smith, in January 1851, that he had come to accept Smith's argument that the Constitution be interpreted as an antislavery instrument. He confessed that he had grown weary of agreeing with slaveholders and their friends that slavery was legal and proper within the Constitution. By May 1851 Douglass had moved into close enough accord with Gerrit Smith to entertain his proposal for the merging of the *North Star* with the *Liberty Party Paper.* He was now prepared "to treat Slavery as a system of '*Lawless violence*' incapable in its nature of being legalized," ready to correct the legal interpretations of the Consitution to make it conform to the principles of the preamble. He could now accept the efficacy and the morality of political action as a weapon against slavery.

Less than a month after Douglass informed Smith of his change of mind, he had occasion to tell his New England friends. The eighteenth annual meeting of the American Anti-Slavery Society was held in Syracuse in late May. A resolution was put before the convention that several papers, including the *North Star,* be recommended by the society. Garrison objected that one of them—the *Anti-Slavery Bugle*—supported the Liberty party and did not deserve their endorsement. Douglass then stood to explain his own change of position, that he now saw the Constitution to be consistent with an antislavery interpretation and was urging political action and voting on his readers.

Garrison was outraged. Implying that Douglass had been bought off, he insisted "there is roguery somewhere," and moved that the *North Star* also be removed from the list of approved papers. The motion carried, and while there had been a chill in their relations since Douglass had decided to publish the newspaper, from this moment on he was to be one of Garrison's "enemies."

The Garrisonian press subjected Douglass to a torrent of abuse. He was said to be not only wrongheaded, but lacking in gratitude for the support his friends had given him in the past. They would never accept Douglass's change to be one of principle. At worst, it was unmitigated opportunism, abandonment of principles for promises of support from advocates of political abolition. The very best they would say was that he had fallen under evil influences of "enemies" like Gerrit Smith and Julia Griffiths. As for the lady, Garrison wrote that she was "one of the worst advisers ... whose influence over him [Douglass] has not only caused much unhappiness in his own household, but perniciously biased his own judgement."

At the next annual meeting of the American Anti-Slavery Society, Douglass presented himself to the convention and demanded to know why he was treated as an alien there. The Garrisonians were quick to tell him: he had abandoned principle. He was accused of "avarice, faithlessness, treachery, ingratitude." Stephen and Abby Kelly Foster told him that they would work to win supporters away from his paper since they did not consider it wholly antislavery. Douglass defended himself, but there was no removing the bitterness. He suffered attacks against him in the *Liberator* and the *Anti-Slavery Standard,* and had to get used to seeing his editorials reprinted in the *Liberator's* "Refuge of Oppression" column as if they were *proslavery* commentary.

It was not until December 1853 that Douglass made a public response to the attacks on him. He devoted six columns of *Frederick Douglass' Paper* to reprints of these criticisms and twelve columns in answer to them. He tried to be calm and reasoned, but he could not avoid personal charges and bitterness of his own. According to Douglass, the dispute came down to one thing: the Garrisonians could not tolerate honest difference of opinion. He was especially offended, however, that Garrison would make his home and family the subject of public discussion. He charged Garrison with condescending to blacks and holding in slight regard their role in the struggle against slavery, quoting him as denying that blacks had any ability *"as a class,* to keep pace ... or to perceive ... or to understand the philosophy" of the antislavery cause.

Douglass was troubled by the charge of opportunism, perhaps because there was an element of truth in it. The circumstances of the merger with the *Liberty Party Paper* coinciding with the public announcement of his change of opinion was suspicious. He made sure, therefore, to point out that his mind had been open to change for over a year.

William Lloyd Garrison would not be generous. To him and his followers it seemed that Douglass had simply gone where he could get the most. Maria Weston Chapman had worried when Douglass was in England that he might be lured away by money. For the suspicious, there was enough circumstantial evidence to convict him. Douglass's defense was a futile effort. Douglass and Garrison were never again to speak as friends, and most of the New Englanders never forgave him for what they considered his ingratitude.

Douglass's conversion to political abolition made sense on a number of counts. The question of extension of slavery into the territories acquired in the Mexican cessions added an important new element in the struggle against slavery. Those who wanted to maintain the western lands as "free soil" were organizing politically to combat slaveholder interests. Theirs would be a popular and viable political issue. Moral suasion and disunion was beginning to have less appeal to blacks as their position seemed only to deteriorate after over a decade of moralizing. Furthermore, as Douglass came to see it, No Union with Slaveholders merely avoided complicity with evil; disunion, if brought about, would free no slaves. There was little difference, in this respect, between the disunionism of Garrison and the emigrationism of Martin R. Delany. Both would abandon slaves to their Southern masters as long as they could live free of the blight. Douglass came to reject disunion, as he had emigration, as self-serving and not in the slave's interest.

Accepting the political path, however, meant compromises; about that Garrison was right. It meant accepting allies whose principles, moral ferver, and program priorities differed from one's own. Douglass quickly discovered that to be political meant to seek the possible rather than the ideal. He followed the shifting political sands of the 1850s, coming to terms with men whose views were far from his own.

Quite naturally, Douglass had begun as a supporter of the Liberty party, which had an unequivocal stand on slavery. In 1848, however, he attended the Buffalo convention of the newly formed Free-Soil party, which would merely restrict slavery from the western territories. Despite its limited platform, Douglass was enthusiastic about the potential size and breath of the new party, and urged his readers to vote for Martin Van Buren and Charles Francis Adams.

In 1852 Douglass was still ambivalent, editorializing in favor of the Liberty party but serving as secretary to the Free-Soil convention and finally supporting its candidates, John P. Hale and George W. Julian.

By the election of 1856 the political ground had changed a great deal. The Kansas-Nebraska Act of 1854 had shattered old party alignments. Northern Whigs, antislavery Democrats, and Free-Soilers came together in Ripon, Wisconsin in 1854 and founded the Republican party. Originally, the Republicans called for the repeal of the Kansas-Nebraska Act and the Fugitive Slave Law, and demanded the abolition of slavery in the District of Columbia. By 1856, however, they had retreated, asking only that slavery be restricted from the territories.

Again, Douglass was ambivalent. He confessed to being tempted by the promise of success the Republicans offered, but he saw in this "the grand corrupter of all reforms": the appeal of a large, popular party for which "we are at liberty to abandon everything."

By August, however, he came to see the Republicans as something more than the "heterogeneous mass of political antagonism" he had called them. In supporting John C. Frémont and William L. Dayton, he was not endorsing the party as it stood, but, as he apologetically wrote Gerrit Smith, "we have turned Whigs and Democrats into Republicans and we can turn Republicans into Abolitionists."

When the Republicans, meeting in Chicago, selected Abraham Lincoln for their standard bearer in 1860, Douglass was not surprised. True, except for his reputation for unblemished character, Lincoln was an unknown and untried figure. True, the Republican platform was even more backward on slavery than the one in 1856 had been. But Douglass had become resigned to political realities. He was not disappointed that Lincoln had won out over New York's William Seward. In trying to make himself accessible, Seward had backed down from what had been a fairly radical position of seeing slavery and freedom as locked in an "irrepressible conflict." In a Senate speech early in 1860, he had studiously avoided any echo of his earlier adherence to "higher law" doctrine and demands that the Supreme Court rescind the *Dred Scott* decision. He had become more conciliatory, speaking of disagreements over slavery as being "political, not social or personal differences." To Douglass's mind, Seward had earned his defeat by trimming.

Douglass had few illusions that the growing popularity of Republicanism reflected conversions among Americans to abolition. Some Republicans opposed slavery because they thought it uneconomical and inefficient; some because it elevated an aristocratic class which despised labor; some because the slave interests constituted a power which would impose its sentiments, ideas, and practices on the entire country; and some because of the fact "that white men have an aversion to blacks, and that introducing blacks into the new territory, practically amounted to the exclusion of whites."

In the campaign of 1860 Douglass tried to persuade the Republicans to strengthen the abolitionist element, to make it the major part of their campaign. "Teach the people for once in a political campaign the sacredness of human rights, the brotherhood of man, and expose . . . the foul and terrible abomination of Southern slavery, and your Republican party will deserve success, which is even better than success itself." He would take them as they were, however; he could do no better. The party, after all, had its origin in the Liberty party, formed twenty years earlier. That party had been swallowed by the Free-Soil party, and that, in its turn, had been swallowed by the Republican party. The original genius was abolition, he reasoned, and so, with resignation, Douglass would support Lincoln in the hope that the seed would in time shape the mature growth.

One the eve of the election of 1860 Douglass was gloomy about the prospects for the antislavery movement. Thirty years of intense labor had nearly succeeded in enlightening the public to the enormities of slavery, but there were few practical results. The moral conscience of the public had not been aroused. "The grim and bloody tragedies of outrage and cruelty are rehearsed day by day to the ears of the people, but they look on as coldly indifferent as spectators in a theatre." Most, it seemed, accepted as factual the representations of slavery by abolitionists, accepting also the "iron-linked logic and soul-born eloquence of Abolitionists," but remained unmoved to act on principle or emotion. Every effort of mind and heart had been expended "to arouse the callous hearts of the American people," and yet four million remained slaves.

Strangely, he remarked, all of Europe was "rocking and heaving with the struggle for liberty, while America is comparatively indifferent under a system of bondage more terrible than Europe has known for centuries." Garibaldi could land in Sicily with a few hundred men, and a "generous and appreciating people" flocked to his standard to "drive the tyrant of Naples from his bloody throne." But John Brown, who took up arms against "a system of tyranny more cruel and barbarous than that of the murderer of Palermo," was hanged in Virginia "while thirty millions of people, whose civil catechism is the Declaration of Independence, look on unmoved to interference."

He did not believe that Americans were lacking in appreciation of liberty or courage. The paradox remained, however, that slavery was sustained by those who could call themselves republicans and free men. The reason was, he believed, that "our patriotism is intensely selfish, our courage lacks generosity, and our love of liberty is circumscribed by our narrow and wicked selfhood, that we quietly permit a few tyrants to crush a weak people in our midst." The central feature of American character was self-interest, a "wicked selfishness," that provided no fulcrum for the lever of justice and humanity. Eager and quick in the defense of their own rights, Americans were indifferent to the plight of those whom they oppressed. "Heaven help the poor slave, whose only hope of freedom is in the selfish hearts of such a people!"

But then he knew that heaven would be of no help to the slave, "except by moving him to help himself." Freedom for the slave would have to come from his own effort to free himself. Self-reliance was the answer, after all. "Outside philanthropy never disenthralled any people." It had taken Spartacus, himself a Roman slave, to lead an army of slaves against Roman legions. So, too, he wrote, "the slaves of America await the advent of an African Spartacus."

There was, he thought, something latent in the American character that respects a rebellious Spartacus over a moral but submissive Uncle Tom. American sympathy quickens to the heroism in defense of liberty. How eagerly they welcomed the patriots cast up from "the wrecks of European revolutions." When some African calls the slaves of the South to arms, and "inspires them to fight a few desperate battles for freedom, the mere animal instincts and sympathies of this people will do more for them than has been accomplished by a quarter of a century of oratorical philanthropy." He regretted that appeals to "higher and better elements of human nature" had failed. But so it had. And the slave had either to await the moral and cultural evolution of the American character or rebel; "did they know their strength, they would not wait the tardy growth of our American sense of justice."

He knew that Americans would be shocked at his call for slave rebellions, but he puzzled at the curious attitude that would applaud the use of bayonets to overthrow European tyrants and "shudder and cry peace at the thought that the American slave may one day learn the use of bayonets also."

He had come a long way from moral suasion, and he was no longer quite sure of the political process either. He could not stir up much enthusiasm for the Republicans. He served with a convention of radical abolitionists to nominate Gerrit Smith and Samuel McFarland, but he had little heart for such political gestures. He worked hard to change the New York constitution to gain an unrestricted franchise for New York blacks, but the equal suffrage measure was voted down by more than a two-to-one margin. He tried valiantly to salvage something positive from the election of 1860. The Lincoln victory, however slight were the gains for abolitionism, did show the possibility of electing "an *anti-slavery reputation* to the Presidency."

That was really slight comfort, and it became less so as the Southern movement toward secession caused Northern, Republican-controlled legislatures to repeal personal liberty laws which had protected fugitive slaves, and engendered new attacks on antislavery people and their meetings. Lincoln's inaugural address did not help. While Lincoln rejected compromises which would appease secessionists, he promised to leave slavery untouched in states where it already existed. He promised the strict enforcement of the Fugitive Slave Law. He would preserve the Union. Those who would advance the cause of the slave and free black people could find little to applaud in that.

For the first time, Douglass's despair seemed to make him consider emigration as a reasonable alternative. He planned a trip to Haiti, to sail on April 25 in order to see for himself what the possibilities were and report to his readers. But the events of early April and the firing on Fort Sumter on April 12 caused him to change his plans. Here was a likely revolution in all that would affect the lives of black people. He would wait and watch developments, "and serve the cause of freedom and humanity" in any way he could. Maybe, he speculated, Northern people could be moved to make war on the slave power. "At any rate, this is no time to leave the country."

IV

# Liberty *or* Union

Along with most Americans of his time, Frederick Douglass had a providential view of American history. It had been no accident that the continent became available to Europeans when it did. Human progress was being marked out in the new-world settlement, and in the United States one could find a nation breaking free from the corruption and tyranny of the old world, founding itself on natural law. It had been in God's design to give men, at a precise moment in history, a vision of the divine ordinance and a chance to realize it in the United States with its Declaration of Independence as the expression of natural law, the Constitution should have translated its ideals and principles into republican institutions suited to a divine purpose.

Many Americans articulated this sense of providence in expansionism under the slogan Manifest Destiny, in which superior Anglo-American institutions were to be brought to the service of other peoples in the hemisphere. Most, however, saw this ordained progress as ideational rather than territorial. It was for the American nation to be true to its ideals and create a society in which all men could live in prosperity and peace. The promise of America was the perfectability of society and the perfectability of man in the creation of the ultimate in social evolution: a Nation of Nations.

Douglass, like most black leaders, held to this view of America seeing a special providence in the presence of the African in America. God would not have suffered such an enormity as the slave trade were it not ultimately to serve some higher end. Some, with a missionizing turn of mind, saw that ultimate purpose to be the return of the Afro-American to Africa to bring Christianity to a pagan people along with the benefits of civilization. Douglass, however, saw it differently. The African was the ultimate test of American civilization. The American had a higher calling: to achieve the will of God in this world. But to do that, he must see the sin against God of slavery and racism and accept the Afro-American as a man, a citizen, and a brother. Only then could the American civilization come into its own.

Douglass's faith in the righteousness of this view, in the essential moral capacity of every man, and in the certainty that evil would not go unpunished sustained him in the long, arduous, and frustrating struggle against slavery and racism. A people, no matter how arrogant and self-assured, could not for long work against the laws of God and nature without retribution. The American people had good and evil before them in the starkest of terms: the idealism of the Declaration of Independence and the unmitigated evil of slavery. All of human history might well be seen to have led to this dramatic confrontation. To be uncertain of the outcome was to be faithless in divine design and purpose.

The events of the 1850s sorely tried Douglass's certainty of a guiding providence. The coming of the Civil War revived his faith, not so much in people as in the power of historical forces to resolve contradictions. No one wanted it but the war came. Northerners, and even Republicans, had seemed willing to give up any worthwhile principle, ignoring human rights, for peace. Nevertheless, the war came.

Antislavery advocates had been predicting a crisis of union all along. The fundamental contradictions of a free society resting on slave labor had bound Americans in a logic of events that had to lead to this point. Even a Southerner, Hinton Rowan Helper, had come to see by 1857 that slavery was necessarily destructive to Southern society. While his book,

*The Impending Crisis of the South,* was an economic rather than a moral critique, it nevertheless predicted a crisis. The view of inevitability was echoed in William H. Seward's rhetoric, the "irrepressible conflict," and even in Abraham Lincoln's "house divided." The war, when it came, seemed merely to bear out what Douglass had known all along: the laws of nature and the logic of events would lead to this unless Americans willingly took the radical path, abolishing slavery and combatting racial prejudice.

War changed everything. The Garrisonians, who had advocated disunion and nonresistance, were curiously drawn to support of the war to defend the Union. Black emigrationists, like Martin R. Delany, convinced themselves the war would make the United States a suitable place for Afro-Americans. Douglass saw the war as vindicating his main position: the wrong of slavery would be paid for in the blood and anguish of the nation. But the war could not be allowed merely to take its course; the issues needed to be correctly understood by national leaders, and the prosecution of the war had to be pressed unrelentingly toward the eradication of slavery.

There was little in Abraham Lincoln's conception of the war and its issues to cheer Douglass. True, Lincoln had been fast in his refusal to compromise with secessionists, and he had been firm in holding to the Republican party's policy on exclusion of slavery from the territories, but he would have left the slave to his master and the fugitive to his fate with slave hunters. Lincoln would hold to no principles more compelling than the Union itself. For those, like Douglass, who had never found virtue in a union based on slavery, Lincoln's position could inspire little confidence.

Douglass saw his role as bringing the nation to see the war as against slavery and for freedom, and to bring blacks, both slave and free, into the war as active combatants. Although he would be frustrated and annoyed at the slowness of Lincoln, he remained convinced throughout that the war would be revolutionary, and would itself be the best educator of conservative leaders.

Seeing the war as a means to end slavery, Douglass was anxious that it be carried at once into the heartland of the South. He had always seen the four million enslaved blacks as the Achilles's heel of the American nation. With the South's secession, the vulnerability was the Southern Confederacy's alone. The quickest way to end the rebellion was to strike at the South's vitals, to arm the slave and free black volunteers, and the Confederacy would be bound to collapse at once. Knowing that Republicans like Lincoln had as Whigs and Democrats been able to accommodate themselves very well to slavery in the Old South, he was fearful that unless blacks became a part of the war, Northern and Southern conservatives would make a peace that left the status of blacks unchanged.

Abraham Lincoln would have had it that way if he could. He was unwilling to view the war as inevitably revolutionary. He believed that he could best save the Union by raising no challenges to existing institutions and prejudices. He rested his strategy on the Border States—Delaware, Missouri, Maryland, Tennessee, and Kentucky. Their presence within the Union would be ready proof of the possible coexistence of slavery with the new administration. They represented a moderate alternative to the extremism of secession. As Lincoln understood it, the principle which held border-state moderates to the national government was that of preserving the Union, and only that. To encourage the thought that the government's war had any other end but to save the Union would be to alienate those moderates.

Except for having declared himself against the extension of slavery into the territories (a popular position in Illinois), Lincoln had never been an antislavery man. He had, at the Illinois Republican convention during the heat of the 1858 campaign, come close to arguing an irrepressible conflict between slavery and freedom. That was the implication, at least, of his pronouncement that a "house divided against itself cannot stand." Even so, when accused of abolitionist sentiment by Stephen Douglas, he was quick to say he merely wanted the new territories to be "in such a condition that white men may find a home," not for American whites only but "for *free white people everywhere*—the world over—in which Hans, and Baptiste, and Patrick . . . may find new homes and better their conditions in life." He had committed himself merely to the containment of slavery, sharing the belief of many Northern whites that the United States was a white man's country.

His own ambivalence about slavery was more than sustained in the attitude of generals in the field, whose interpretation of the war's aims determined the fate of slaves who came within their jurisdiction. Many field generals did not disguise their sympathy for the Southern aristocracy. Some, like George McClellan of the Army of the Potomac, could be accused of devoting more energy to the capture and return of fugitive slaves than to an aggressive pursuit of the Confederate army.

From Lincoln's first call for volunteers, Northern blacks pressed to be enlisted in the Army. Some suggested schemes of using Northern blacks to organize slave revolts. Lincoln, however, had no intention of recruiting black soldiers, fearing both the border-state reaction and a negative effect on Northern white enlistments, using black troops and provoking slave insurrections might be a way to win a war, but it was hardly a way to preserve a white man's Union.

The war, as Douglass saw it, had a momentum of its own and would not be confined to the convenient limits Lincoln desired. Once the die had been cast, once the slave states seceded and the Confederacy had established itself in defense of the slave system, it was futile to look for moderate positions which would have denied Southerners a share in the nation's future on their own terms. In time expediency would force

Lincoln beyond his war of limited liabilities into one that would redefine the nation altogether. But he could not be hurried by Douglass or abolitionists or even radicals within his own government.

The question of the status of fugitives who surrendered themselves to Union officers was an early test of the government's intentions. They were, after all, property under national law, and Lincoln's government wanted in no way to suggest that it questioned the right of ownership of such property. Some field officers, therefore, were conspicuous in returning fugitives. On the other hand, it was clear that the owners of many of these fugitives were in rebellion against the government and that slave labor sustained the Confederate war effort.

General Benjamin F. Butler, while commander of Fortress Monroe in Virginia, declared on 25 May 1861 that the black people who escaped to his lines were "contraband of war" (language which sustained their condition as property) and would not be returned to their owners. Butler's policy was accepted by the government without enthusiasm. On 6 August 1861 Congress passed the First Confiscation Act, which provided for the "confiscation" of slave property used in arms or labor against the United States government. Both Butler and Congress left unclear what would be the new status of this "confiscated contraband." In practice, such fugitives were impressed into labor for the Union army, they could hardly be called free.

General John C. Frémont, commander of Union troops in Missouri, declared martial law in that state on 30 August 1861. He also declared the slaves of those in arms against the United States to be free. His action was much in advance of Lincoln or Congress. Undoubtedly conscious of Frémont as a past and potential political rival, the president was not about to surrender to him leadership in defining war policy; Frémont's order was rescinded.

As 1862 began, the government had not moved very far on the question of slavery. Douglass was disappointed. Beginning in the fall of 1861 his lectures and editorials hammered away at the notion that slavery was the central issue in the "rebellion." It had to be attacked frontally. Throughout the winter and spring of 1862 his message was the necessity for "instant and Universal Emancipation."

He was greatly impressed by a change in public sentiment. His entire career on the public platform had brought him to expect hostility and even violence from white audiences. Now, the hisses and the catcalls were gone, and he was listened to with respectful attention. There was not only a new-found respect but a general acceptance of his central premises: that the evil of the slave power was the root cause of the war, and that a cessation of slavery was necessary to end the war. As he saw it, the Northern public was far in advance of Lincoln and his government; Washington needed to get the message.

Lincoln advanced schemes of compensated emancipation to the Delaware legislature and to representatives from the other Border States in the spring of 1862. He hoped they would agree to a plan whereby slaveowners in those states would be paid for their losses in freeing their slaves. He was rebuffed. Congress, however, approved his plan in principle. On April 16 Congress passed and Lincoln signed into law a bill which abolished slavery in the District of Columbia, compensating the owners of slaves freed by the measure.

Thus, between Congress, military commanders, and the president there seemed little coordination or plan about slavery. On 9 April 1862 General David Hunter proclaimed the emancipation of slaves in his department, which included Georgia, Florida, and South Carolina. As with General Frémont, Lincoln overruled this order. Congress emancipated slavery, without compensation, in the territories on June 19, and a month later passed the Second Confiscation Act which freed the slaves of anyone who "committed treason" or supported the "rebellion." The slaves of such persons, the act declared, "who shall in any way give aid . . . being within any place occupied by rebel forces and afterward occupied by the forces of the United States . . . shall be forever free of their servitude, and not again be held as slaves."

Lincoln's ambivalence toward slavery and his solicitude about property rights caused him to lean toward a veto of the Second Confiscation Act. While he did not follow through, he actually wrote a veto message which argued that the "severest justice may not always be the best policy." He signed the legislation but he transmitted his veto message with it so that it became part of the legislative record.

Lincoln tried to breathe new life into the colonization idea, hoping to remove slaves and free blacks from the country and from consideration in the war and the peace that was to follow. In his first message to Congress, in December 1861, Lincoln recommended colonization for slaves and free blacks. In April 1862 one hundred thousand dollars was appropriated and placed at the president's disposal to colonize those slaves who had been emancipated in the District of Columbia. Although nothing came of it, Lincoln persisted in what had been, for nearly fifty years, a Whig dream: the removal of the problem of blacks and slavery from the country.

On 14 August 1862 Lincoln invited a group of black men to discuss the issue. He wanted them to urge their people to leave the country. New Granada in Central America would welcome Afro-Americans, and he encouraged such a move. He told the delegates that their "race suffer greatly . . . by living among us . . . while ours suffers from your presence." Lincoln's scheme, however, found no better reception among blacks than had all the previous appeals. He persisted, nevertheless, bringing the matter before his cabinet in September, aiming to make treaties with Latin American and European countries. Under Lincoln's urging, Secretary of State Seward circulated a letter among European governments that colonized in the Western Hemisphere, asking their cooperation in resettling Afro-Americans.

Douglass was shocked not only at the government's irresolute prosecution of the war but especially at Lincoln's revival of the chimera of colonization, which he had thought deservedly dead and buried. He responded with angry editorials, charging Lincoln with prejudice and hypocrisy. How else could one explain the president's charge that the war was caused by "the presence of the Negro in America. It was as if a horse thief or highwayman blamed his crime on the presence of a horse or a traveler's purse." Douglass was unimpressed with Lincoln's resoluteness to deal a death blow to Southern rebellion. The Second Confiscation Act had empowered the president to arm fugitives who came within Union lines, but Lincoln shrank from using this means. He would rather indulge fantasies that blacks would disappear into a Central American empire.

Lincoln's flirtation with colonization was more than wishful thinking, however. Postmaster General Montgomery Blair wrote Douglass, urging him to reconsider his opposition to a plan to establish a new empire in Central America of Afro-American immigrants. Blair thought Douglass mistaken in thinking the same assumptions were at the basis of both slavery and colonization. Even Thomas Jefferson had advocated colonization. Racial diversity rather than inferiority made separation of the races desirable; since the races were created different, to separate them was merely to follow God's design. Blacks had to leave because whites had the power, "and it cannot be reasonably expected that they would voluntarily go away." It was expected that with the success of the new empire and the knowledge that blacks could and would migrate, "poor whites . . . will be for emancipation, and . . . the prejudice produced by enslavement of the race will soon die away."

Douglass was quite practiced in answering colonizationists, and there were few new wrinkles in Blair's letter. Men should be free to migrate—black as well as white—but they should not be forced by the pressure of public law or theory. Douglass denied that white men had any aversion to blacks. Had that been so, Europeans would not have invaded Africa and "stolen" her people for labor in the New World. At that very moment, indeed, the white man's face was appearing in Asia and Africa. If Afro-Americans hoped to get away from the Anglo-Saxon by going to Central America, it would be a vain hope. "You may send us to Central America this year, and the white man will be at our elbow next year." White Americans were comfortable exploiting blacks: "For . . . the trouble is that our white fellow countrymen have not yet reached the sublime height of civilization" where "each man is content with his just portion."

Douglass believed, however, that men of different races could indeed live together peacefully. After the adoption of the Constitution, Douglass claimed, black men voted in Virginia and North Carolina. They bore arms in the military under George Washington and Andrew Jackson. He could remember the time when black men served on American warships, "uniformed and treated precisely as other marines." Only the augmentation of the slave power, attempting to extend its reach over Northern as well as Southern states, accounted for the amplified claim that free blacks and whites could not live together.

For him, there was no difference between the defense of slavery and the argument for colonization: "The argument that makes it necessary for the black man to go away when he is free, equally makes it necessary for him to be a slave while he remains here." Douglass reminded Blair that neither he nor any other advocate for colonization proposed the removal of slaves from the United States. No one ever advocated legislation to remove the slave population. Colonization, rather, rested on the vain hope that once free blacks had established themselves somewhere, slaveowners could be persuaded to send their slaves to that place. What seemed beyond the understanding of men like Montgomery Blair was that "it is a standing complaint of the white people of the South that they are legally deprived" of bringing more slaves from Africa.

The emancipation of slaves could not await a viable scheme for the removal of free blacks, for that placed between the slave and his liberty the mountains of expense and difficulties attendant to colonization plans. Solutions might never be found. Colonization, therefore, became "an opiate to the troubled conscience of the nation," retarding the natural course of freedom for the slave.

Whatever Lincoln's dreams of other ways out—that blacks would go away or that moderate Southerners would prevail in the notion that the Union was a value transcending all others—he had at last to confront slavery or give up the war. The military circumstances of the war forced this choice upon him. European governments were tempted to support the Confederacy in deference to their own industrial interests; they could hardly find the cause of the Union compelling. And as the war moved into its second year, Northerners became impatient and resentful of its costs, and the need for decisiveness became imperative.

By July 1862 Lincoln seemed to have accepted the inevitable. On July 22 he announced to his cabinet that he intended to proclaim all slaves free in those states still in rebellion on 1 January 1863. He refrained from any public statement, however, and continued to pursue a course of cautious reserve. He awaited the appearance of a military victory. On September 22, following Robert E. Lee's setback at Antietam, he issued the preliminary proclamation of his intentions.

Making it clear that he had not adopted abolitionist ideas, Lincoln was careful to reiterate in the proclamation that the purpose of the war was the restoration of the Union and that he intended still to work for compensation for those who voluntarily freed their slaves. He did declare, however, that "the Executive Government of the United States . . . will do no act . . . to repress such persons . . . in any effort they make for their actual freedom," thus removing the confusion of policy toward fugitives within Union lines, and implying an official indifference to slave insurrections. Yet slavery would remain untouched in those states still part of the Union. All of Tennessee was omitted as well as those portions of Virginia and Louisiana that were under the control of the Union army. In fact, the proclamation would do little beyond what Congress had done in the Second Confiscation Act.

Douglass was in no way deceived that Lincoln's edict would actually break the chains of any slaves. He was saddened by the grudging way the president came to do what Douglass knew to be right; he had done the deed "like an ox under the yoke, or a Slave under the lash." Douglass noted that Lincoln had delayed for three months the effect of his proclamation, presumably still willing to leave slavery untouched if Southerners were willing to lay down their arms. And in his annual address to Congress on December 1 Lincoln gave every sign that he hoped to be excused from the obligation to fulfill his pledge.

Despite these reservations, Douglass told his readers that they would witness a momentous day on January 1. Lincoln could not go back on his word, and the Confederates would give him no excuse to back out. Once that edict took effect, the "national ship" would be swung around into "the trade winds of the Almighty." It could never turn back and live. The proclamation would add "four millions to the strength of the Union, . . . establish the moral power of Government," and kindle anew the enthusiasm of the friends of freedom. The war would be based at last on the defense of freedom over slavery —the only grounds on which it credited a people and a nation to struggle.

On the night of December 31 Douglass took part in a vigil at Tremont Temple in Boston. There were over three thousand in the audience awaiting official word from Washington. The old abolitionist crowd was there. There were speeches by Douglass, J. Sella Martin, the black preacher William Wells Brown, a fugitive from slavery, and Anna E. Dickinson, the women's rights advocate. It was well after ten at night before a man came through the crowd, yelling, "It is coming! It is on the wires!" The crowd erupted in cheers; there were prayers of thanksgiving, and the joyous celebration spent itself only with the dawn.

January 1863 was a month of jubilee celebrations for blacks across the country, and Douglass traveled over two thousand miles speaking at gatherings from Boston to Chicago. He reflected deeply on recent events; one of his first childhood questions had been why black people were slaves, and he had wondered if they would be forever. "From that day onward, the cry that has reached the most silent chambers of my soul, by day and by night has been How long! How long oh! Eternal Power of the Universe, how long shall these things be?" Now, it seemed, the handwriting was on the wall.

The use of black troops in the Union army followed the Emancipation Proclamation. The edict announcing that freed slaves would be received into the army was not clear how they would be used. Early in 1863 Congress passes a resolution authorizing the enrollment of blacks into the military service.

As early as April 1862 General David Hunter, commanding the Department of the South, had organized a regiment of black troops from fugitives in the area. After several months in camp, however, these men were sent off without pay by order of the War Department. Once Lincoln's proclamation was announced in September, sentiment and army policy changed. In November Thomas Wentworth Higginson, the Massachusetts abolitionist, was asked to command a regiment which would be the first unit of former slaves in the Union army. In September General Benjamin Butler, commander of Louisiana, began organizing three regiments of infantry and one of artillery from the black men of that sector. The next month, General Augustus Chetlain organized several regiments of black volunteers in Tennessee.

The government had yet to provide a means for Northern blacks to serve. Governor John A. Andrews, of Massachusetts, asked permission to raise two regiments of black troops. The War Department gave him authorization to enlist volunteers, including "persons of African descent, organized into separate corps." So, in late January 1863, Governor Andrews announced the formation of the Massachusetts 54th Regiment, the first black unit to be recruited in the North. It would be very difficult to fill the Regiment's roster from Massachusetts residents alone, so Governor Andrews called upon Frederick Douglass, who was eager to help.

For Douglass the martial role for blacks was crucial. If the war could be waged without regard to black men, slave and free, then there could be little argument about the justice of their oppression. He knew that only by black involvement could abolition become the chief war aim. The more blacks participated, shifting the balance, the more they could be certain of affecting their future.

He published his stirring editorial, "Men of Color to Arms," which was to be reprinted in newspapers throughout the North and used as a way to encourage recruitment. He urged black men to put aside their questions about the duplicity of the government and its tardiness in calling them. The time had come and black men must enlist: "Liberty won by white men would lose half its luster. 'Who would be free themselves must strike the blow.' " He called cowardly that cynicism which dismissed this as the "white man's war," which claimed that blacks would be "no better off after than before the war." This was the hour of black men, and they must act. "I am authorized to assure you," he wrote, "that you will receive the same wages, the same rations, the same protection, the same treatment, and the same bounty, secured to white soldiers." The entire reputation of the race rested upon the willingness of black men to take up arms. "The chance is now given you to end in a day the bondage of centuries, and to rise in one bound from social degradation to . . . common equality with all other varieties of men." He called to them in the spirit of the black insurrectionists who had given their lives for liberty: Denmark Vesey, Nat Turner. He did not forget Shields Green and John Copeland who had followed John Brown.

In March Douglass began a recruiting tour of western New York. His sons, Charles and Lewis, were among the first to join the Massachusetts 54th. But Northern black men were not automatic recruits; they could point to little in their experiences with white men and the government to give them confidence or a sense of loyalty. The decade of the 1850s followed by Lincoln's mean and grudging spirit had nearly shattered their morale as citizens. Douglass hammered away, nevertheless, at the necessity for them to act as citizens whatever others would have them be. Popular predudice considered them cowardly and unmanly; manhood required them to serve in the army. White Americans would deny them citizenship; only by assuming the responsibility of citizens could they rightfully challenge that denial. The rights of black men were in question; learning the use of arms was the surest way to claim and defend their rights. Oppression and prejudice had undermined black men's self-respect; enlistment and martial valor would regain it. An army of black men, in the final analysis, would be the best guarantee against a "pro-slavery compromise at the end of the war." Douglass had fair success in his efforts. By the end of May, the all-black 54th Regiment sailed from Boston harbor for South Carolina.

Douglass found, as he continued his recruitment efforts, that he was more and more embarrassed by the disparity between his assurances to black men and the realities of their army service. Despite Governor Andrews's word and the efforts of white officers like Thomas Wentworth Higginson, black troops, when they were paid at all, were paid as laborers rather than than as combat troops. They suffered insults and harassment at the hands of Union army officers and men. When captured by the Confederate army, they were treated as slaves and fugitives rather than as prisoners of war. They were denied honors they had earned, and they were not promoted into commissioned ranks.

From the beginning Douglass had warned that black troops

would suffer annoyances: their mistakes amplified, and their successes ignored. But he had believed that their valor, despite these abuses, would triumph over both slavery in the South and prejudice in the North. He had not been prepared, however, for systematic discrimination, purposeful and official insult by the Union army and the government.

There came reports of Confederate atrocities against black soldiers, and the national government did nothing. The story was that Confederates refused to treat black troops by the conventions of war. Jefferson Davis had, on 23 December 1863, declared that slaves captured in arms would be treated as felons rather than as prisoners of war. Prisoners wounded in battle had little chance of surviving, and others were likely to be sold into slavery rather than imprisoned. Word of massacres was everywhere to be heard. Some were untrue, but others, like the shooting of twenty noncombattant teamsters at Murfreesboro, were genuine. The horror stories multiplied with reports of new engagements in which blacks played a major role: Port Hudson, Milliken's Bend, Fort Wagner. Still there was not even a word of official protest from Washington. How different it had been when two white officers had been threatened with execution at Richmond; the national government promised to retaliate and nothing happened. For Douglass it was an old story, recalling to him his youth in slavery. The saying went: "Half a cent to kill a Negro and half a cent to bury him." In protest Douglass ended his recruitment efforts.

He informed Major G. L. Stearns, the man charged with recruiting blacks for the Massachusetts regiment, of his grievances. Stearns urged Douglass to go to Washington and lay his complaints before the president. Through Stearns an audience with Lincoln was arranged for early August.

Douglass could not have helped being awed by the momentous and symbolic character of his meeting with the president. Twenty-five years had passed since his escape from slavery; his beginnings in bondage remained sharply etched in his mind. His sense of personal obligation to those who remained in chains was never more keen than during the war years. As a free man he had been reminded at every turn that he and his people were despised by the vast majority of white Americans. Even this president, with whom he was to talk, had shown no sign that he did not share in that general contempt. And yet the audience with the president marked the distance he had traveled from servitude to public celebrity.

There was more here than pride of personal accomplishment, although there was that too. Douglass, from his first days as an antislavery speaker, understood himself to be—both in his own view and that of those who looked on—a representative of his people. Representative, not in his being a typical black man or a spokesman for a cause, but in that his very person and life symbolized the black American inspiring respect. Thus, his meeting with Lincoln was fraught with meaning far beyond the specifics of their discussion.

Any apprehension he may have had about how he would be received was quickly put to rest. He was admitted at once on presenting his card. Lincoln rose to greet him, shook his hand, and put him at his ease. He was direct and frank with Douglass, but in every way treated him with respect. The president was neither officious, patronizing nor condescending; that went a long way with Douglass. "Honest" was the word that came to his mind to describe the president. Thus, he found some satisfaction in an interview which on every other score was disappointing.

Douglass urged three matters on the president. Black soldiers should receive the same pay and bounties as white soldiers. The government should protect black soldiers as readily as whites; they should be exchanged as prisoners the same as others, and protected from inhuman treatment; and the United States government should promise to retaliate the murder of captured black soldiers. Finally, he asked that distinguished and valorous service by black soldiers be rewarded as with white soldiers and that promotions, including commissions, go to those so deserving.

Lincoln answered that the use of black soldiers had not been a popular move, that unequal pay seemed to him a necessary concession to smooth the way over popular prejudice. In time, he promised, the pay would be equal. In any case, he argued, black people had more to gain from their service in the army than others and might be content to suffer for a time a difference in pay. He confessed that he did not know what to do about Confederate treatment of black soldiers. While he deplored their policy, he could not bring himself to the kind of retaliation that would arbitrarily hang some Confederate soldier who was at hand for the deeds of those out of reach. He did promise, however, to sign any commission recommended by Secretary of War Edwin M. Stanton.

Lincoln gave no ground in the interview. Even on the matter of commissions he had not said that he would instruct the War Department to commission black officers. Governor Andrews had been given to understand that neither Stanton nor Lincoln were ready to make black commissioned officers. Lincoln had no intention of standing in advance of what he thought to be white public opinion on race. But Douglass came away satisfied with the character of the man, his honesty and humanity. Douglass's faith in what he called the "educating tendency" of the war, that events would pull Lincoln and the nation further than they dreamt of going, persuaded him to take up once again his recruiting efforts.

There were, in fact, some tangible changes. On July 30 Lincoln issued an order stating that for every Union prisoner killed in violation of the rules of war, a Confederate prisoner would be similarly executed; and for every Union soldier enslaved or sold into slavery, a Confederate soldier would be put to hard labor. He had been slow to act, but he acted. Douglass, before the December meeting of the American Anti-Slavery Society, quoted the president as saying: "remember that Milliken's Bend, Port Hudson, and Fort Wagner are recent events; and that these were necessary to prepare the way for this very proclamation of mine." Lincoln may not have been willing to engage in the fact of retaliation, but he seemed ready to use the threat of it; this mollified Douglass and other black men.

After leaving his interview with Lincoln, Douglass met with Secretary of War Stanton, who again defended his department's treatment of black troops on what were now familiar grounds. He did make Douglass a very attractive offer. Early in March Stanton had given General Lorenzo Thomas the command of recruitment in the lower Mississippi Valley. He invited Douglass to join Thomas in the recruitment and organizing of black troops. He offered him a commission if he would accept the work. Douglass quickly agreed.

He returned to Rochester and threw himself into preparations for this new role as officer in the Union army. There was pride involved, of course, but he had also come to believe that "the true course to the black man's freedom and citizenship was over the battlefield," and that his business was to get every black man into the Union army.

It meant that he would have to close down his paper, but he had little regret in doing that. He had kept it going for sixteen years, accomplishing what he had set out to prove: that a black man could publish and edit a paper of high quality. His columns and opinions were now welcomed in newspapers like the New York *Independent* and the *New York Tribune,* each having circulations mounting to one hundred thousand. There were other lively black newspapers, like the *Anglo-African.*

Douglass was undoubtedly weary of the month-to-month struggle to print the paper and keep it solvent. Sooner or later he would have to let it go. What better time than at the height of the war, and what better way than to take up a military commission. So, on 16 August 1863 Douglass wrote his "valedictory" editorial, and with that August issue, *Douglass' Monthly* ceased publication.

The commission never came. Douglass waited, ready to go, but the War Department never came through. Douglass wrote to inquire, but there was never an explanation or even an acknowledgment that a promise had been made him. He was merely instructed to go to Vicksburg and report to General Thomas. Stearns wrote to inform him of his salary, but without the commission Douglass would not go.

Aside from his personal disappointment, the matter only reminded him how frightened still the government remained of racist public opinion. Stanton apparently did not feel the public was ready to see a black man as an assistant adjutant. It strengthened Douglass in his belief that it would be a mistake to leave the future of black people in the hands of such a cautious and uncommitted leadership. The full weight of black people had to be felt, and the most immediate way to assure that was to fill the army ranks. He continued to work at doing that, though as a civilian rather than as a Union army officer.

By the end of the war some 200,000 black men had served in the Union army and navy. Whatever Lincoln's words to Douglass meant, very few of them became officers during the war. General Benjamin Butler had commissioned seventy-five in the three regiments he raised in 1862, but most of them were replaced by white men under General Nathaniel P. Banks. At the end of the war, six sergeants of the Massachusetts 54th and 55th Regiments were promoted to lieutenant. An independent Kansas light-artillery battery had three black officers. Eight black surgeons were commissioned as majors, and in February 1865 Martin R. Delany was commissioned Major of Infantry and ordered to recruit an *"armée d'Afrique"* in South Carolina. Excluding chaplains, not more than one hundred blacks received commissions during the war.

Throughout the war, Douglass was deeply torn. He saw the administration as inclined to hedge on principles having to do with black people. Failing the press of expediency, Douglass knew that blacks would be left high and dry by Lincoln and his government. Yet Lincoln was all they had, and Douglass knew he was better than many they might have. At least he seemed to have a personal integrity. Douglass remained persuaded that the events of history had a way of carrying men beyond themselves. The war was an opportunity for black men to shape its aims and determine their future as well. Shakespeare's words came to his mind, and he never tired of quoting them:

> There is a tide in the affairs of men,
> Which, taken at the flood, leads on to fortune.

He stressed to his audience what to him was the real message of these words:

> We must take the current when it serves
> Or lose our ventures.

Thus, he was circumspect in his criticism of the Lincoln administration lest his words reinforce the cynicism of alienated black men. Understandably, many wondered how they would profit from serving a Union whose most fervent hope was to be a white man's country.

Cautious as he was, he could have no illusions. Lincoln continued to entertain colonization notions in thinking ahead to the end of the war. The conciliatory policies of General Nathaniel P. Banks, who, in December 1862, replaced General Benjamin Butler at New Orleans, suggested the quasi slavery that would certainly follow hostilities if matters were allowed to drift. Lincoln, himself, had already given signs that he would welcome Southerners back into the Union with only token signs of loyalty, promising nothing in the way of rights and power to those blacks who dared the wrath of their masters by service to the Union. With 1863 coming to an end, the unexpected length of the war and its awful cost began to take its toll on Northern white sentiment. There was every reason to fear that the government and the people lacked the resoluteness to finish a war to end slavery if some accommodation short of that could be found. As Douglass saw it, only the steadfastness of the Confederacy kept the war going at all. If exhaustion opened them to compromise, the cause of the black people would be cast aside.

Douglass hoped at this point to rally the old antislavery forces. The danger was they would become complacent now that "disunion" was a fact of war and that the Emancipation Proclamation had made slavery legal only in those states loyal to the Union. He spoke to the annual meeting of the American Anti-Slavery Society in December 1863. His message was that their work was far from ended. As they had formerly struggled to bring the enormity of slavery to the public mind, they must now work to make a Republican reality of the Democratic charge that it was an abolitionist war. He reminded his friends that their Achilles's heel was color prejudice in the North. They must protest against it and expose it. For as long as black men and women are kicked off street cars in Philadelphia, black soldiers paid less than their white comrades, there would be the danger of compromise. The public needed to understand that lasting peace depended on the freeing of all slaves and the enfranchisement of blacks throughout the country. The necessity of this last point was not felt by many in his audience, but Douglass stressed it and would continue to do so.

Frederick Douglass framed a speech, the "Mission of the War," which he first delivered at New York's Cooper Institute in February 1864, and which he was to repeat throughout the North in the following months. It was his most thoughtful analysis of the conflict and its prospects for the nation and for black people.

He warned against the delusion that slavery was now dead, providentially killed by the fact of war, and against the appealing cliché that revolutions never go backward. The war might well prove the nation's ruin if the issue of freedom and justice to black people was not firmly grasped. If a revolution was in the making, he had yet to see the evidence for it. Like the recent government upheavals in Europe, this struggle, too, he said, might result in little change at all.

He could understand the impatience and gloom that pervaded the North. What had been predicted to be a ninety-day war was going into its third year. The human cost had mounted to over 200,000, the debt incurred by the war was like "a mountain of gold to weight down the necks of our children's children." But the fearful thing was that the public might rush to a peace of accommodation leaving fundamental issues untouched, setting the stage for resumption of conflict at a later time.

It was no surprise to him that Democratic party members, now calling themselves men of peace, were charging the Republicans with conducting an abolitionist war. To Douglass's chagrin, the Republicans found this embarrassing. The Democrats, he charged, had for thirty years supported slavery: in the war with Mexico, in the annexation of Texas, in the Fugitive Slave Law. They found no principle in the right of *habeas corpus* when it came to fugitive slaves, or in states' rights when it came to personal liberty laws, but they supported such principles in the cause of the Confederacy and its Northern sympathizers. To Douglass, the Democrats' call for peace was treason pure and simple. Yet, the Democrats' subversion troubled him less than the Republicans' duplicity and irresolution: "We have much less to fear from the bold and shameless wickedness of the one than from the timid and short-sighted policy of the other."

The truly loyal man, in Douglass's view, had to take an uncompromising stand on four points: that the aim of the war was the abolition of slavery; that there would be "consent to no peace, which shall not be . . . an Abolition peace"; that everyone in the country be entitled to the same rights, protection, and opportunities; and, since the white race should have "nothing to fear from fair competition with the black race," that black men should be invested "with the right to vote and to be voted for."

As yet neither Lincoln nor the Republicans had come to accept even the first two planks of this platform, and Douglass must have known that even his abolitionist friends would shrink from putting their support behind the third and fourth. To his mind, Lincoln's public statements were in no way different from those of the late Stephen Douglas, who expressed indifference if slavery were voted up or down. Yet it was a deception to fancy the reestablishment of the Union, for "that old Union . . . we shall never see again while the world standeth."

The war had to be fought for a new kind of national unity, not shamed by slavery, not belying the Declaration of Independence, in which patriotism would not conflict with justice and liberty, in which sections and sectional interests would be erased.

The new nation he envisioned would transform the South so that the "New England schoolhouse" takes the place of "the Southern whipping-post." We want a country, he said, "in which no man shall be fined for reading a book, or imprisoned for selling a book . . . where no man may be imprisoned or flogged or sold for learning to read, or teaching a fellow mortal how to read"; that liberty, freedom, and national unity had to be the object of the war or else it would be little better than a "gigantic enterprise for shedding human blood."

The war, he thought, might be a part of the nation's Manifest Destiny, forcing a reorganization and a unification of the country's institutions into a true national unity; not a union but a nation. He felt a divine energy at work, for it was only as the government took its grudging steps in the direction of liberty had "the war prospered and the Rebellion lost ground." Humanity and justice did not win at each moment; they were often overpowered. But "they are persistent and eternal forces" against which it was fearful to contend. They constituted a force in nature, and the rulers had only to "place the Government fully within these trade winds of Omnipotence," and the Confederacy would be doomed.

Antislavery work was never more needed. "The day that shall see the Rebels at our feet," he said, "will be the day of trial." The moral character of the nation would then be tested, and it would prove true to its calling only if it held firm on the essential issues: "No war but an Abolition war; no peace but an Abolition peace; liberty for all, chains for none; the black man a soldier in war, a laborer in peace; a voter in the South as well as in the North; America his permanent home, and all Americans his fellow-countrymen."

With such a sense of the "Mission of the War," Abraham Lincoln's policies continued to trouble Douglass. Early in 1864 his discontent with the president was most intense. He wrote to English friends hoping they would help expose from abroad the shame and *"the swindle"* of the government's abolitionism. The administration's policy remained to *"do evil by choice, right by necessity."* Lincoln, he noted, was presently to pocket veto the Wade-Davis Bill, which would have restricted the organization of Southern state governments to those with a "loyal majority." The president preferred his own plan which called for only ten percent. Douglass warned his English friends that Lincoln had no intention of extending the franchise to blacks in the South. He thought it dishonorable to invest rebels with political power and hold it from those loyal to the government: "To hand the Negro back to the political power of his master."

There was little to hearten Douglass in the spring of 1864. Horace Greeley, the idiosyncratic editor of the *New York Tribune,* responding to the general peace sentiment of the moment, agreed to meet at Niagara Falls with two Southern emissaries claming the authority to seek openings for peace. Greeley asked Lincoln's support, and the president wrote the editor on July 9 promising to meet "any person, anywhere, professing to have any proposition of Jefferson Davis in writing for peace, embracing the restoration of the Union and the abandonment of slavery."

As it turned out, the Southerners intended merely to engage in peace agitation in the North and were not genuine peace emissaries from the Confederacy. Greeley had unwittingly been used by them and was responsible for false hopes and much confusion. Lincoln, hoping to clarify his own position, made public a letter addressed "To Whom It May Concern" in which he reiterated the language in the Greeley letter. He would welcome any proposition which "embraces the restoration of peace, the integrity of the whole Union, and the abandonment of slavery."

Aside from the administration's embarrassment over the Greeley peace fiasco, Lincoln came under fire because of the contents of his letter. Copperhead Democrats made much of the fact that Lincoln had made the "abandonment of slavery" a condition of peace. A people who had been called to war to preserve the Union were being obliged to continue it until slaves were freed. Moderate Republicans, sensing that the president had shifted the ground on which the war was being fought and unwilling to defend an "abolition war," quickly made their differences public and began pressuring Lincoln to recant.

Late in August the troubled president, on his own initiative, invited Douglass for a second audience. He had heard of the black man's growing criticism of him and his administration of the war, and he wanted his advice on two matters.

The first issue concerning the president stemmed from the public's reaction to his "To Whom it May Concern" letter. Lincoln had drafted a response stating that no legitimate proposal of peace had come to him, and he was not, therefore, standing in the way of peace. He would make it clear, as well, that he could not sustain, on his own, a war for the abolition of slavery if Congress and the people would not support it. In other words, his proposed letter would deny himself the power to do what his critics accused him of doing: blocking peace by making abolition a condition. Asked his opinion of this letter, Douglass strongly advised against Lincoln answering his critics at all, and certainly not with a letter which might be construed as abandoning an antislavery policy. Influenced by Douglass or not, Lincoln did not publish the letter.

Lincoln's second concern was far the most troubling to Douglass. Fearful that the war might end without the defeat of the Confederacy, and doubtful of the legality of the Emancipation Proclamation, Lincoln wanted Douglass's opinion as to how to speed the flight of slaves from their masters to the Union lines. He saw it as a way of weakening the enemy, but also expressed to Doulgass the fear that only those who *"succeeded in getting within our lines would be free after the war was over."* Douglass gave thought to the problem, and in a letter dated August 29 sketched out a plan suggestive of John Brown's original scheme for helping slaves escape.

The gloom in Washington was thick. There was no sign that the Confederacy was weakening. Indeed, the Capitol had been shaken by Jubal Early's thrust at Washington which brought Confederate troops almost within sight. With it all, the administration was facing a national election which might well turn the Republicans out.

Earlier, Frederick Douglass had given his support to a call by radical Republicans and abolitionists for a convention to oppose the renomination of Abraham Lincoln. The convention met on May 31 in Cleveland, nominating John C. Frémont for president and John Cochrane, a nephew of Gerrit Smith, for vice-president. The platform called for the uncompromised prosecution of the war, a constitutional amendment to prohibit slavery, a one-term presidency, postwar reconstruction by Congress rather than the executive, and the confiscation of Confederate lands to be redistributed to loyal soldiers and actual settlers.

On 8 June 1864 the Republican, under the name of the National Union Party, met in Baltimore. They nominated Lincoln to stand for reelection and Andrew Johnson, the War

Democrat from Tennessee, for vice-president. There was no great enthusiasm for Lincoln, but the party had little alternative. The platform and public statements from the convention carefully disassociated the party from any identification with abolitionists or the cause of black Americans.

So matters had stood in August when Douglass met with the president. He was certainly no Lincoln supporter at that time, but he would change. Perhaps he was flattered a bit that the president called on him for advice; undoubtedly he sympathized with his dilemma. But it was the results of the Democratic party's convention in Chicago that made the difference. Meeting in August, the Democrats nominated General George B. McClellan for president on a peace platform. The party was ready to concede that the war to save the Union had been a failure, and demand only that "immediate efforts be made for the cessation of hostilities." Douglass, and most other abolitionists, learning of the Chicago convention, shifted their support to Lincoln. "All dates changed with the nomination of McClellan," he wrote. General Frémont, himself, was persuaded to withdraw from the race.

Early in October 1864 the first convention of black men to meet in a decade opened in Syracuse. It was attended by 144 delegates, representing seven slave states. Douglass was named president of the convention and wrote its "Address to the People of the United States." The document resonated the urgency of the moment. For now not only did black people have to contend with their traditional enemies and public complacency, but even the Garrisonian press—the *Anti-Slavery Standard* and the *Liberator*—were divorcing themselves from demands for the enfranchisement of blacks.

Douglass's argument stressed the importance of political equality for blacks in the South. All that slaves may gain in freedom could be taken away without the vote. Consider the European immigrants, said Douglass. It was neither their virtue, their knowledge, nor their wealth that gave them consequences in American eyes. It was that "our institutions clothe them with the elective franchise, and they have a voice in making the laws of the country." The black American must have that power as well, or many would cease being slaves to individuals only to become slaves to the community.

The convention came out in support of Lincoln, and urged blacks and white friends to vote for him. Douglass, in fact, volunteered to speak for the Lincoln candidacy, but the Republicans were hesitant to associate with this black abolitionist. So Douglass stayed out of the campaign.

Throughout August it seemed there would be a Democratic victory. Indeed, Lincoln wrote a formal memorandum outlining his proposed role during the interim between the election and the inauguration in the event of a Democratic victory at the polls. But in early September the tide of war turned clearly in the Union's favor. Atlanta fell to General Sherman on September 3, giving Lincoln the military victory he sorely needed. He was reelected handily.

After the election Douglass again took up the lecture circuit. Now, with the collapse of the Confederacy imminent, he could extend his tour into regions he never before dared go. He went into Virginia for the first time, and he gave six lectures in Baltimore. This "homecoming" was a personal triumph to Douglass as a free man of stature and repute. His visit was also the occasion of an emotional reunion with his half-sister, Eliza, who in the thirty years since last he saw her had managed to buy her freedom along with that of her nine children.

Abraham Lincoln was assassinated on April 15. Frederick Douglass was among those to eulogize him. Most black Americans had come to look upon him as a great president and a friend to black people. However far that was from the truth, and however grudgingly he moved to support the interests of Afro-Americans, they would join in his celebration as the Great Emancipator.

Douglass, of course, knew better. He had been one of the president's severest critics while he lived. He knew that Lincoln did very little for Afro-Americans, slave or free, and that what he did was grudging, calculated, and expedient. He may well have become educated to a more generous view of Afro-Americans had he lived, and Douglass would not be wrong in seeing himself as the president's educator. But surely Douglass would have preferred several other men to Lincoln. And he knew that had the president lived to serve out his term, there would be nothing in his program of reconstruction to applaud. Lincoln would not have been an advocate of suffrage for the freedman or any other major reform in the South. Chances were that he would continue flirting with colonization schemes or encourage plans to make freedmen wards of the community.

Yet, Douglass eulogized him, attributing to the dead president qualities which he had found lacking in the living one. And Douglass was not alone. As a martyr Lincoln could be a more effective reformer than he would have been in life. If one could identify him with the cause of freedom and justice for the black man, one could go a long way toward claiming principles in his name which he would hardly have staked his life or career on.

In the spring of 1865 Frederick Douglass played his part in the creation of the Lincoln myth. As is so often the case with myths, this one came to have more vitality than the real man. In time Douglass came to forget there was a difference.

V

# Citizen Douglass

FOR DOUGLASS, peace meant nothing less than recognition of citizenship rights for Afro-Americans throughout the country. He found it convenient to ignore the fact that the white American public and the national leadership had never really accepted his definition of the war's purpose. In the flush of military victory, it might be possible to expand and enlarge their vision.

Douglass was certain that justice was on his side, but there was more. Slow and circuitous as was the Union was in acting, it had come to grant freedom to the slaves of the Confederacy; that had been the telling blow. Grudging and deceitful as the Union was in accepting black troops as combattants, by the war's end there were 200,000 black men in federal uniforms; these men had been crucial to the Union's victory. Inadequate as Abraham Lincoln had been while alive, as a martyred president he embodied all the ideals of humanity and racial justice; the myth was inspirational. The Republican party had been callous to Afro-American interests from its beginnings, but success as a postwar, national party demanded a broader constituency with perhaps the black voter as its major strength. Douglass would exploit such lines of argument.

The fight for peace would be as difficult as the war itself, and Douglass set out to caution friends against relaxing now that the South was defeated.

Early in 1865, speaking before the annual meeting of the Massachusetts Anti-Slavery Society, he stressed the urgency to organize and to act. The drifting policy, like that of General Nathaniel Banks who had worked to undermine a limited black franchise in Louisiana and who had used his command to force freedmen to labor for planters under terms set by former slaveholders, seemed certain to return blacks to a modified slavery rather than to freedom. There needed to be a national policy in which the federal government would completely transform and democratize the South.

The keystone of the new order would be universal suffrage. Douglass called for the "immediate, unconditional, and universal enfranchisement of the black man, in every State in the Union." Now was the time, with the costs of the war heavy on the American conscience, and the lessons of the war fresh in their minds. Otherwise centuries might pass before the moment would again be ripe. The franchise was crucial to blacks because it was their right. In monarchical systems, Douglass pointed out, class and rank were normal and the lower orders suffered no special odium for being denied privileges of the aristocracy. To be denied fundamental privileges in a republic, however, was to be excluded from citizenship itself.

The very strength of the nation, Douglass argued, now depended upon blacks getting the vote. The spirit of rebellion remained in the hearts and minds of former slaveowners, intensified by the pain of defeat. Southern hostility would continue to subvert the nation until the "rank undergrowth of treason" had been rooted out. Meanwhile, the nation's vitality would rest on that group whose loyalty came from sentiment and self-interest: the freedman.

Furthermore, the nation was honor bound to protect the freedman in his right to vote. By relying on black soldiers, it committed itself to their future. Southern blacks had been asked to support the Union and its government, to incur "the deadly hate of the entire Southern people, to abandon the cause of their masters and take up the cause of the North." Now, Douglass asked, do "you mean to give your enemies the right to vote, and take it away from your friends?"

As in their struggle for freedom, blacks would have to rely on the abolitionists. Douglass knew, however, that it had been easier for his old friends to work for freedom than it would be for suffrage. The one was a clear moral issue calling upon their philanthropic spirit. Conferring the vote would be the granting of power. The American people, Douglass observed, were disposed "to be generous rather than just." Everywhere in the country could be seen the signs of philanthropy toward the freedman. There were educational societies, sanitary commissions, and freedmen's associations, all reflecting a kind of benevolence. Even General Nathaniel Banks's misguided policies might have stemmed from a philanthropic sentiment to "prepare" the freedman gradually for responsible citizenship. However well-meaning, these were not what was needed. "What I ask for the Negro," he stressed, "is not benevolence, not pity, not sympathy, but simple *justice.*"

Such justice would be found only in the power of citizenship. The black man should stand on his own feet or fall. "Let him alone," was Douglass's prescription. He did not need benevolence and interference, and if he required these for survival, he should be allowed to die. White men had indulged themselves in a number of deceptions about the black man, and their philanthropy reflected it. They had supposed that he would not fight; the war disproved that. They imagined he would not work; with freedom it would be shown that he would "work as readily for himself as for the white man." The best thing his friends could do for him would be to protect him in his right to be independent.

The April meeting of the Massachusetts Anti-Slavery Society had opened a breach among the Garrisonians. Wendell Phillips had stood with Douglass in the demand for the immediate enfranchisement of the freedman. William Lloyd Garrison was opposed. As he pointed out, blacks were still denied the ballot in Connecticut, New Jersey, Pennsylvania, and several western states; it would be unfair to impose on the South what the North itself had not come to accept. The Phillips-

Douglass position carried over the Garrisonians' objections. Again, with Phillips and Douglass speaking against him, Garrison had moved that with the achievement of emancipation, the society's work was done and should be dissolved. Again, the old leader was defeated.

Garrison opened the May meeting of the American Anti-Slavery Society with a resolution calling for the dissolution of the society. It was an "absurdity" to maintain an antislavery society after slavery was dead. Phillips and Douglass again objected. Slavery was not dead. The Thirteenth Amendment prohibiting slavery had yet to be ratified by the states. Slaves were, in fact, legally held in the United States. That amendment, they pointed out, in no way guaranteed citizenship rights to blacks. Until that was done, there was plenty for the society to do.

The vote on Garrison's resolution was 118 to 48 against him, and he saw himself abandoned by the movement he had done much to establish. With some bitterness, Garrison resigned from the society along with those who sided with him. By the end of the year, he closed the files of the *Liberator,* feeling that the work he had set out to do was finished, and he watched from the sidelines as Wendell Phillips and Frederick Douglass led those who would follow into postwar reform.

Douglass's program of reconstruction had two essential features. Controls were needed to keep the old-line Southern leadership from rapid return to power; demonstrated loyalty to the national government should be essential. Since the "rebellion" had been led by the "slave power," the best sign of loyalty would be the acceptance of emancipation, its justice as well as the fact of it. Unless assurances were had, the old leadership would sustain the spirit of rebellion and reestablish slavery in fact, if not by law. Secondly, former slaves had to have political power to protect their status as freedmen, to be a force in the liberalization of the South.

Douglass was quite aware that Northern black citizenship was as much at stake as the freedom of slaves. If that moment was not grasped, Northern blacks would very likely continue in their anomalous status. He even presumed that the reconstruction following the war would of necessity be national rather than regional, expecting a change in federalism such that the central government would define the character of citizenship for all people throughout the nation. He did not flinch at the thought of weakening traditional states' rights; he welcomed it.

The reconstruction policy of Abraham Lincoln had rested on far different assumptions. Lincoln had wanted to reestablish "normal" relations with the former Confederate states as quickly and as easily as possible. His Proclamation of Amnesty and Reconstruction of 8 December 1863 would have pardoned any former Confederates who would take an oath swearing to support the Constitution of the United States. He excluded from this amnesty high-ranking officers in the Confederate army and navy, those who resigned commissions in the United States in order to serve the Confederacy, and those who left judicial and congressional posts in the United States in order to serve the South.

He further stipulated that when, in any Southern state, persons numbering one-tenth of the votes cast in the presidential election of 1860 had taken the oath and established a new state government, he would recognize that government as part of the Union.

Black men were no part of this process. Lincoln seemed to want to establish governments as closely approximating those of the antebellum period as possible, given the facts of war and emancipation. When, in February 1864, Louisiana successfully followed this plan, electing Michael Hahn as the first postwar governor, Lincoln wrote Hahn to "barely suggest, for your private consideration, whether some of the colored people may not be let in, as, for instance, the very intelligent, and especially those who have fought gallantly in our ranks." That was as far as Lincoln would go on the question of the franchise for blacks.

Andrew Johnson probably thought of himself as carrying on Lincoln's program. Lincoln had appointed him in 1862 military governor to oversee Reconstruction in Tennessee. At first, he spoke as if he would be tougher on the Confederacy than the late president would have been. He told Senator Benjamin Wade, and any who would listen, that "treason is a crime and crime must be punished. Treason must be made infamous and traitors must be impoverished." A number of radical Republicans, including Charles Sumner and Thaddeus Stevens, were convinced that Johnson shared their views on Reconstruction and would defer to Congress as Lincoln had not. They were quickly disabused as Johnson, during congressional recess, recognized the the governments of Arkansas, Louisiana, Tennessee, and Virginia. All of these state governments had been organized under Lincoln's plan. He then proceeded to grant amnesty to Confederates who took an oath of allegiance; he made an exception of those holding taxable property exceeding $20,000. So, it would seem, he was out to get the wealthy. Even such persons, however, could petition him personally, asking for special pardon, which he was liberal in granting.

Johnson quickly moved to organize the remaining seven states. Provisional governors were empowerd to convene conventions of "loyal" citizens (including those pardoned by the president) to amend the state constitutions, abolish slavery, and repudiate the war debt. By December 1865 all the Confederate states except Texas had complied. In his first message to Congress on 6 December 1865 Johnson could declare that the Union had been restored; the delegates of the ex-Confederate states merely awaited admission to Congress.

Douglass had predicted that an easy restoration of the Confederate states would, in effect, mean a returning of the exslave to the control of his former master, and he was right. Beginning with Mississippi, the former slave states enacted a body of vagrancy and apprenticeship laws holding blacks to the land and severely restricting their freedom and civil rights.

These "black codes," the unchecked violence against blacks, and the general elevation of former Confederate political leaders to office substantiated his claim that the South would remain unchanged if the old crowd were allowed to regain power.

Blacks had good reason to be troubled by Johnson's solicitude to former Confederates, and sought to bring their concerns to the president's attention. Douglass, his son, Lewis, and three other black men had an audience with Andrew Johnson on 7 February 1866. It was a respectful, even deferential delegation, referring to Johnson as "your Excellency." It was, nonetheless, clear and purposeful in its expressing its point of view.

George T. Downing, a successful Washington caterer, spoke for the group. The recently ratified Thirteenth Amendment, prohibiting slavery, was by itself not enough, he declared. There was a need for supportive legislation protecting blacks in their rights as citizens. Recalling how the *Dred Scott* decision had left matters, Downing was anxious to assert: "We are citizens; we are glad to have it known to the world that you bear no doubtful record on this point." He pressed upon the president the view that there was "no recognition of color or race in the organic law of the land. It knows no privileged class." He hoped, therefore, that blacks would be enfranchised everywhere in the country, for their fate could not be left to those who would "outrage our rights and feelings." The war had shown that the national government "may justly reach its strong arm into States" demanding allegiance. May it not at this time, he asked, "reach out a like arm to secure and protect its subjects?"

Douglass followed Downing, pointedly remarking on the accidental nature of Johnson's presidency and the consequent obligation to honor Lincoln's commitments. "In the order of Divine Providence," he said, "you are placed in a position to save or destroy us . . . I mean our whole race. Your noble and human predecessor placed in our hands the sword to assist in saving the nation, and we do hope that you, his able successor, will favorably regard the placing in our hands the ballot with which to save ourselves."

Andrew Johnson's response was a characteristic rambling, but there was no mistaking his meaning. He felt no need to apologize for any lack of humanity or "feeling for the colored man." He had owned slaves himself, but he had always felt he was enslaved to them. "For the colored race," he insisted, "my means, my time, my all has been perilled." So he confessed to considerable annoyance at being "arraigned by some who can get up handsomely-rounded periods and deal in rhetoric, and talk about abstract ideas of liberty, who never perilled life, liberty or property."

As a friend of the colored man, he did not want to adopt a policy that would end in a "contest between the races, which if persisted in will result in the extermination of one or the other." What was needed, Johnson declared, was a practical and common-sense approach. The black American needed a Moses. If he could find none better, he said, "I would be his Moses to lead him from bondage to freedom . . . I would pass him from a land where he had lived in slavery to a land (if it were in our reach) of freedom." But he would not willfully adopt a policy which would result in the shedding of the black man's blood and the loss of his life.

The president reminded the delegates that he had opposed slavery, but on two specific grounds: it constituted a great monopoly in the hands of a few, making them an aristocracy holding power over those who did not hold slaves; it was also objectionable in principle. As he saw it, it was the white majority, the nonslaveholding class, who were tyrannized by the slave system. Slaves, in fact, generally held themselves to be superior to nonslaveholding whites, he claimed. In this way slavery had created, according to Johnson, a natural enmity between blacks and white democracy.

The war, the president insisted, had been fought to put down a rebellion, not to free slaves. The abolition of slavery came "as an incident to the suppression of a great rebellion." In that sense, blacks had gained from the war while non-slaveholding whites had lost life and property. Those who survived the war had gained nothing, but lost a great deal.

By giving political power to blacks, he suggested, one would be degrading the status of poor whites. Was it just, he asked, to place whites "in a condition different from what they were before?" Clearly, Johnson would call it unjust.

He would consider extending the franchise to blacks only where a majority of white consented to it. Properly, the franchise was a state matter to decide; it would by tyrannical to impose on a people what they did not want. "The people," for Andrew Johnson, were white people. The government was derived from them, and it was only they who could justly extend the power of government to blacks. The fact that they were unlikely to do it did not change things or place the issue in the president's hands. Even if he thought differently, he could not presume, he said, to be "wiser than Providence, or stronger than the laws of nature."

Respectfully, Douglass offered some points in rebuttal of the president's argument. He suggested that given the vote, Southern blacks and poor whites could establish a party strong enough to contend with the Southern aristocracy. Johnson, however, had given all the audience he intended. On leaving, Douglass said to his fellows, "The President sends us to the people." And Johnson answered, "Yes sir; I have great faith in the people. I believe they will do what is right."

On leaving the president, the delegation met with some congressional Republicans and reporters. The story of the interview appeared in the *New York Tribune* on February 12. Douglass, in the name of the delegation, wrote an open letter to the President which was published in the *Washington Chronicle.* In it he gave the rebuttal that Johnson had refused to hear.

Douglass argued that whatever hostility existed between blacks and poor whites had been the result of slavery and the slaveholder's calculated setting of the one against the other, better to control them both. It was illogical to base postwar policy on the assumption of the continuation of such antagonism. But even if racial hostility did continue into the era of freedom, it contradicted Johnson's professed concern for the black man to "deprive him of all means of defense, and clothe him whom you regard as his enemy in the panoply of political power."

Racial peace, he insisted, would not come by "degrading one race and exalting another," by giving power to one and not the other, "but by maintaining a state of equal justice between all classes." The president, Douglass wrote, should not entertain the colonization or emigration of blacks as a solution. There would never be a time when blacks could be removed from the country "without a terrible shock to its prosperity and peace. Only the worst enemy of the nation," he continued, "would argue that Negroes could be tolerated . . . in a state of the most degrading slavery and oppression, and must be cast away, driven into exile, for . . . having been freed from their chains."

By such criteria, Andrew Johnson himself was an "enemy of the nation." In commenting to his private secretary, Gideon Welles, the president minced no words as to his opinion of the delegation and his cleverness in handling them. "Those damned sons of bitches thought they had me in a trap," Johnson said. But they could not deceive him. "I know that damned Douglass; he's just like any nigger, and he would sooner cut a white man's throat as not."

In "going to the people" against Andrew Johnson, Douglass and his friends were not alone. The 39th Congress, when it convenied in December 1865 did not accept President Johnson's view of Reconstruction and refused to seat representatives from the states which had conformed to his formula.

Congress began to wrest Reconstruction from the hands of the president. They established the Joint Committee of Fifteen, dominated by such radical Republicans as Thaddeus Stevens and Charles Sumner. They at once set out to expand the powers and extend the life of the Freedmen's Bureau, which had been established in March 1865 to administer abandoned lands and the accommodation of freedmen to their new life. Johnson vetoed the bill, holding that Congress, without representation from eleven states, lacked power to legislate and that the bill's provisions for military trials violated the Fifth Amendment. On 16 July 1866 Congress passed the Freedmen's Bureau Bill over his veto.

Congress also passed a Civil Rights Bill over Johnson's veto. This act was an effort to countermand the dictum of the *Dred Scott* decision by formally bestowing citizenship on persons of African descent and granting to all persons born within the United States, except for Indians, equal civil rights. In this case, Johnson's veto message had denounced the measure as an unwarranted invasion of states' rights. Having doubts of their own on this score, the Joint Committee of Fifteen formulated the Fourteenth Amendment.

Here, for the first time, citizenship would be defined in the Constitution, and that definition would include Afro-Americans. The amendment would also grant the protection of the national government to individual citizens, guarding them in their rights against denial or invasion by state power. Supplanting the three-fifths provision of the Constitution, the Fourteenth Amendment would have all persons counted equally for purposes of taxation and representation; it would reduce proportionately the representation of those states that denied suffrage "except for participation in rebellion or other crime." It would abrogate the public debt of the Confederacy and deny any claim for losses due to the emancipation of slaves. The Fourteenth Amendment was passed by Congress on 16 June 1866 and sent to the states for ratification. Expecting the upcoming congressional elections to repudiate the radical program, the Southern states, except for Tennessee, rejected the amendment.

Everyone seemed ready to go to the voters. Johnson's supporters, through the National Union Club, called a convention of Democrats and conservative Republicans to "sustain the administration." They met in Philadelphia in mid-August, pledged to uphold states' rights in matters extending to the franchise, and denounced congressional reconstruction as "unjust and revolutionary." The radical Republicans called a convention of loyal Southern Unionists to meet in Philadelphia in order to denounce the doctrine of state sovereignty. Although this was a convention of Southerners, Northern representatives were invited as honorary delegates. The New York Republicans, convening in Rochester, named Frederick Douglass as one of their delegates.

Republicans, however, were not yet radical enough to associate themselves publicly with blacks as political equals. Even the archradical Thaddeus Stevens was embarrassed by the naming of Douglass as a delegate. Fearful of public reaction which might cause them to lose congressional seats in marginal districts, the Republican leadership exerted considerable pressure on Douglass to convince him to stay away from the convention. Such ambivalence about race was on old story. He believed their fears to be groundless, and he knew that to accept their argument would be to repudiate the very premise on which he had always stood: blacks were citizens and should be equal participants in the political process.

Not only did he attend the convention, he made his presence felt. At a public meeting he expanded on his views on proper racial policy at that crucial juncture in American history. With Anna E. Dickinson, the women's rights advocate, and Theodore Tilden, the publisher, Douglass was able to persuade the convention to support the extension of suffrage to blacks. If the voters were being asked to choose, at least the issues should be clear between the Republicans and Andrew Johnson.

In late July William Slade, acting for the president, wrote Douglass to inquire into his willingness to replace General O. O. Howard as head of the Freedmen's Bureau. For a black man, a former slave, to head a government agency with a staff exceeding two thousand would have been incredible. With the right policy and effective administration, the bureau could go far toward giving the freedman political and economic power in the South. William Slade's letter stressed the need to replace Howard, describing him as "timid" and lacking in "moral courage." Although he admired Howard, Douglass could see some truth in that characterization, and he knew that local officers of the bureau protected the freedmen's interests according to their personal views. Howard seemed unable to enforce a uniform policy. It took little to convince Douglass that a firm and purposeful leadership was needed. Probably, cleverness was the last attribute Douglass would have granted to Johnson, yet the president placed him in an awkward position.

Andrew Johnson's duplicity was obvious. Had Douglass accepted, he could hardly expect support from a president who had vetoed the legislation establishing the bureau. Without his support, Douglass would have been at the mercy of a staff of white men—doubtless resentful of his authority—many of whom had attitudes about class, race, and the capacity of the freedmen at wide variance from his own. Furthermore, to accept such a post from Johnson and place himself thus under the president's aegis would have compromised Douglass's alliance to the radical Republicans.

He wrote Slade that he could not accept the position if offered. Everything about his letter, however, suggested how much he had been tempted. Without pronouncing on the character or fitness of General Howard, he wrote, that his "present views of duty" obliged him to say no. Yet, he did not close the door altogether. He asked Slade to keep him informed of the direction of the president's thinking, for should he appoint a black man to head the bureau, that would do more than anything he had done to "demonstrate his purpose of being the Moses of the colored man in the United States." If the offer of office would only come from the Republicans, that would be a different story. Douglass threw himself into the work of helping them into power.

As early as January 1866 Douglass had begun an attack on Johnson and his program, but with the congressional elections coming up he began his work in earnest. He was shrewd in separating Johnson from the martyred Lincoln. Speaking on "The Lesson of the Assassination," he characterized Lincoln as progressive—moving forward, never backward—and, by the time of his death, Douglass claimed, the dead president had come to accept a limited form of enfranchisement for blacks in the South. Lincoln, he insisted, had grown with his trials and with the developing crisis. In contrast, Johnson would go backward, honor "traitors," reestablish in the South the very regimes that had been the cause of the nation's pain.

He shared the assumptions and arguments of the radical Republicans. All were calling for a much more demanding program for reincorporating the former Confederate states, and all were pointing with shame at the clear fact that the governments organized under Johnson's plan were different neither in personalities nor in spirit from the Confederacy itself. Many of the radical Republicans were motivated by a vindictive spirit which hoped to see the Southern leadership suffer for the pain of the war. Douglass differed from them in this respect, wanting only to be assured that slavery was dead forever and that blacks would be empowered with the vote. In order to do this, as he saw it, there needed to be a stringent, indeed a revolutionary, program for the South. For the moment, therefore, he and the radical Republicans would use a common rhetoric, but they were masking differences which were real and lasting.

Andrew Johnson stumped hard against the radicals, but he had a lot to overcome. The Democrats still bore the onus of their Copperhead past: being for a compromise peace on the very eve of victory. The Southern governments organized under Johnson, having elected ex-Confederate leaders to office and having passed the "black codes," seemed unregenerate. Vigilante groups, such as the Ku Klux Klan, had begun in the winter of 1865–1866 to beat, harass, and murder blacks and their white friends. There had been bloody riots in Memphis and New Orleans in which black men, women, and children were brutally assaulted and many killed. Events belied Johnson's claim that his approach would lead to racial peace and would be in the interest of black people.

The fact that Southerners were unchanged gave credence to the fear among many northeasterners that a Democratic victory would result in the undoing of much legislation on tariffs, banking, and internal improvements—always opposed by Southerners—which had been passed while Southerners were not in Congress.

By all odds, however, Johnson's greatest handicap was a mean and querulous personality which antagonized and alienated his audiences. The public, therefore, despite his faith in them, repudiated him at the polls. In the fall elections, the Republicans gained two-thirds majorities in both houses, giving the radicals effective control over Reconstruction.

Unhampered by fear of veto, Congress proceeded with its own program of Reconstruction. It placed the Confederacy under martial law, dividing the region into five military districts. It required that new constitutional conventions be called; that the delegates be chosen by universal manhood suffrage. The new governments must guarantee suffrage to blacks and ratify the Fourteenth Amendment. Ex-Confederates, as identified in that amendment, were to be disqualified as voters. Congress reserved to itself the right to review all cases where there was uncertainty, to approve of elected representatives, and to end military rule. This was the core of radical Reconstruction.

Douglass, however, remained uneasy. Slavery was ended and, with certain ratification of the Fourteenth Amendment, blacks were to be declared citizens, protected in their civil rights by the national government; and Congress, unhampered by Andrew Johnson, could guarantee that the new Southern governments would be representative of blacks as well as whites. Still, the right to vote rested on dubious ground. It was being imposed by Congress on Southern states as a condition of their readmission to the Union. Undoubtedly, white hostility would run deep for years to come, and a persistent effort to frustrate Congress's intent could be expected. Furthermore, states' rights advocates challenged congressional power to extend the franchise since suffrage had always been a state matter. Who could say that blacks would not find themselves, sometime in the future, deprived by the Southern states of their right to vote? One could hardly depend on a continued national will to protect them in that right.

Douglass also knew that the South was only a part of the problem. He had always insisted that any meaningful revolution would have to eliminate the institutional effects of racial prejudice in the North as well as end slavery in the South. The power and the rights of citizenship had to be extended to Afro-Americans throughout the country. Nothing in the postwar amendments had affected the citizenship rights of Northern blacks. New Jersey, Connecticut, Pennsylvania, and the western states deprived blacks of the right to vote. Most also placed severe limitations on their residency and rights to hold property. New York, Douglass's home state, imposed special property qualifications on black voters. It was imperative, therefore, while the national mood was right and the reform movement at its peak, to work for a constitutional amendment actually granting the franchise to blacks and depriving any state of the right to restrict it on the ground of "race, color, or previous condition of servitude."

Uncertainty about the future viability of the Republican party caused many of its members to support the idea of such an amendment. After all, the Republicans had gained power as a minority, sectional party. Lacking a broader constituency than they had in 1860, there would be little hope of surviving. How could the party develop strong Southern support? A major premise of Douglass's argument for the amendment was that, especially in the South, the most certain and most logical supporters of the new order would be Afro-Americans. Interpreting "loyalty" to mean loyalty to party rather than to cause or principles, many Republican politicians found themselves in accord with Douglass.

For those who might have had doubts, the presidential election of 1868 brought the message home. The Republican ticket of Ulysses S. Grant and Schuyler Colfax won over the Democrats, Horatio Seymour and Montgomery Blair, by a sizeable electoral vote of 214 to 80. They had a popular majority, however, of only 306,000 out of 5,715,000. Since the black vote in that election exceeded 700,000, it was obviously decisive. What Douglass had argued as a matter of right and justice became for many Republicans an issue of expediency. On 27 February 1869 the Fifteenth Amendment passed in Congress; it was ratified a year later.

The struggle for the Fifteenth Amendment had its price, rending an old reform alliance. The leadership in the women's rights movement, resentful that the amendment would not extend the vote to women, were openly hostile to it. From Seneca Falls, Douglass had been a strong and constant supporter of women's rights and women's suffrage. His old friends, Susan B. Anthony and Elizabeth Cady Stanton, would now ask him to make a single cause of suffrage for blacks and women. Knowing that to do so would be to lose everything, Douglass refused.

During the war, the women had submerged their reform interests to serve the nation, working with the sanitary commissions and women's loyalty leagues. With the war over, they were ready to press their cause anew. They were not willing to accept Douglass's claim that it was "the Negro's hour," and that his rights had to be secured first. They were also conscious that this could be their moment, and, failing to seize it, could mean a loss of decades in their fight. For Anthony and Stanton, the rights of women were no less compelling that those of blacks. As early as 1867, while stumping in Kansas, they had been willing to compromise their stand on the franchise for blacks in order to gain support for the vote for women. Some women in the movement found it especially ironic that the "ignorant black man" should be given the vote before the "intelligent and cultured" white woman.

In May 1869 at the annual meeting of the Equal Rights Association, Douglass stressed the special urgency of the vote for black men. The issue of blacks' political power was different from that of women's. "When women, because they are women, are dragged from their homes and hung upon lampposts; when their children are torn from their arms and their brains dashed upon the pavement; when they are the objects of insult and outrage at every turn; when they are in danger of having their homes burnt down over their heads; when their children are not allowed to enter school; then they will have the urgency to obtain the ballot." White women, at least, he argued, had access to political power through their fathers, husbands, sons, and brothers. Blacks, he pointed out, lacked even that.

Someone in the audience pointed out that the black woman was victimized in the way Douglass had described, not only the black man. The urgency certainly applied to her, and the franchise should be extended to her sex. "Yes," Douglass agreed, the black woman was so treated, "but not because she is a woman but because she is black." Such arguments, however, were unavailing. The sense of the unfairness of the situation ran deep among the women.

The schism also revealed a racism in the women's movement that had remained latent while the possibility of the franchise was unlikely for either blacks or women. With the movement for the Fifteenth Amendment, however, some wanted to use the fear of black political power as a lever to gain the ballot for women. Lucy Stone was a vigorous antagonist of

Douglass on this issue. She and her husband, Henry B. Blackwell, went so far as to advise Southern legislators that by granting the ballot to women, the combined vote of white men and women would offset that of blacks. With such attitudes, the women's movement could not be brought to support the Fifteenth Amendment. Indeed, before the end of the 1869 convention, they voted to disband the Equal Rights Association and form the National Woman's Suffrage Association, thus separating themselves from the cause of black people.

The break was a difficult one for Douglass. He had been proud of his identification with the women's rights movement. Now he would not speak on the women's platform. Justifying his refusal, he wrote Josephine Griffing that as long as blacks were being "mobbed, beaten, shot, stabbed, hanged, burnt," and are the target of all that is malignant in the North and all that is murderous in the South, their "claims may be preferred by me without exposing . . . myself to the imputation of narrowness or meanness toward the cause of woman." He found the positions of Susan B. Anthony, Elizabeth Cady Stanton, and their followers indefensible. Their principle, as he put it, was that no black man should be enfranchised while women are not. "Now, considering that white men have been enfranchised always, and colored men have not," he wrote, "the conduct of these white women, whose husbands, fathers, and brothers are voters, does not seem generous."

In time, the breach between Douglass and the women's suffrage movement would be closed, and he would rejoin his old friends in their cause. He would not, however, live to celebrate the achievement of the vote for women. It would be another fifty years before that would come to pass.

By the spring of 1870 Douglass had reason to feel pleased with the nation's accomplishments. Three constitutional amendments had seemingly secured all Douglass had hoped for. Besides, Reconstruction in the South was safely in the hands of a Congress with a radical leadership. With President Grant, Congress had an executive who would not obstruct its program. It would now seem that the revolution was on its way.

There remained certain problems, of course. The burden of a historical oppression and racial prejudice could not be cast off overnight. Southern whites might for some time require the threat of military coercion. Freedmen would need time and experience before they could function easily as responsible and intelligent citizens. The movement nevertheless, was launched, and as long as the national government remained clear in its purpose and uncompromising in its management of Reconstruction, Douglass was satisfied that all would turn out well.

He had no illusions that pressure and agitation would cease. Habitual attitudes of racial privilege would not be changed by mere law. White men and women would continue to insult blacks, refuse them service in hotels and restaurants, deny them access to schools and colleges, discriminate against them on trains and boats. Workingmen, on their jobs and in their unions, would continue to refuse fair competition with black workers. Race, not merit, would continue to be the touchstone of opportunity. "The divine right of race" would be no easier to overthrow than the divine right of kings. All that was true, but now the terms of the game were different, and Douglass would happily make himself an instrument in the eventual overthrow of more than two centuries of racial tyranny.

Before the war Douglass had shared, at least in part, the Garrisonian view that the nation and the national government was corrupted by the lawful presence of slavery. Even after he had come to accept the Constitution as an antislavery document, he was hard pressed by the Fugitive Slave Act and the *Dred Scott* decision to defend the Union. With the adoption of the postwar amendments, however, all problems and all doubts were cast aside. There could no longer be any question: the Constitution was now a free people's organic law.

Now the United States was a nation to which he could give his allegiance in good faith, a nation to which he could belong.

To belong and be loyal to a deserving nation had been a driving force since his days as a slave. It was a motive quite outside the imagination of such men as William Lloyd Garrison and Wendell Phillips. Douglass's extraordinary effort at self-education, his carefully constructed image of the independent man, his forthrightness, his rationality, his moral integrity had been calculated to show him as the model citizen. He lived his life, even as an agitator and radical, so as to exemplify the perfectibility of the black man and the slave, and to expose the idiocy of a social system that would treat him, and people like him, as pariahs. Each word he uttered, his publishing career, his upright presence on almost any platform for moral reform were clear messages about himself and his people. If anyone should belong and be respected as an American, he should; like him, his people were deserving.

It was not merely a desire to be accepted by white Americans; the America to which he would belong should deserve his loyalty. The nation had to accept the ideals on which it had been founded and strive to live up to them. Douglass's antebellum criticism of the United States was strident and angry precisely because the Union fell so far short of its principles, and because white Americans were so complacent about it. America, however, like humanity, was perfectible, and it was to its dream he would belong.

As the decade of the 1870s opened, the dream seemed well within reach. A new era was dawning; Douglass, and all Afro-Americans, could proudly belong to the new nation. The new era called for a new style and approach. One could now speak of "our country," "we citizens," "our future"; theirs were no longer alienated voices. Belonging meant accepting the result of the democratic process as long as the game was played fairly. Handicapped as they were by lack of education and political experience, blacks could not expect to win all they wanted, or needed, or thought due them. With persistent pressure intelligently applied, however, all would improve with time. Belonging meant compromise and acceptance of an imperfect reality. One could not, as the abolitionists had, insist on perfect justice or nothing. Belonging meant a commitment to the process.

Citizen Douglass was anxious to serve his country as for so long he had served his race. His new attitude caused him to see the entire nation with different eyes. His demands seemed modified and his tolerance augmented.

In January 1871 President Grant appointed him assistant secretary to the commission of inquiry into the proposed annexation of Santo Domingo. He took up the task with great enthusiasm. Joining such prominent men as Andrew Dickson White and Samuel Gridley Howe, Douglass sailed to the Caribbean to investigate social conditions and resources as well as the Dominican people's attitude to the scheme of annexation to the United States. The commission recommended in favor of the proposal.

Their recommendation was no surprise, as President Grant had appointed the commission with his own strong disposition in favor of the plan widely known. Douglass's concurrence, however, placed him in favor of American expansion for the first time; he had been hostile and suspicious of such schemes before the war. In the 1840s he had been a vigorous opponent of Texas annexation and the Mexican War. He had always seen such filibustering as undisguised efforts to expand the slave power. Now, however, in this new national era, he could see such expansion as of "mutual benefit" to the United States and the people of Santo Domingo.

Douglass had been struck by the poverty and the generally low standard of living of the Dominicans. He saw little that was progressive and no evidence of political democracy. The people could not help but benefit, he thought, from the disciplining influence of American institutions.

In supporting annexation Douglass found himself at odds with the radical Republican he admired most. Charles Sumner had been, from the start, the strongest opponent of Grant's plan. Though it was unusual and uncomfortable for Douglass to differ with the Massachusetts Senator, he joined in the commission's recommendation anyway. He was not merely trying to be in harmony with the president's known views, but expressing a genuinely held faith in the potentially progressive effects of the "Saxon and Protestant civilization." He was also aware that annexation would add a sizeable nonwhite population to the commonwealth, fundamentally challenging the assumption of the United States as a white man's country. Some members of the congressional opposition understood this very well.

Always mindful of who he was and what he had been, Douglass was very pleased to have been appointed to the commission. For an American president to put a black man, a former slave, and a known radical in such an office was not only a personal tribute to Douglass but a signal of how far the country had come in matters of race relations. The next such appointment would be easier to make, leading to the time when blacks in public service in the United States would occasion no special notice at all. It was in this spirit that Douglass chose to ignore some racial incidents which, in earlier days, he would never have suffered in silence. On the return trip Douglass was denied dining room service on the small mail packet on which the commission sailed; he was forced to take his meals in his cabin. Although he knew of it, Grant did nothing to censure the officer who was responsible. Three days after their return to Washington, the commission dined at the White House, but President Grant did not invite Douglass. Accepting such slights without public remark was part of the price one had to pay for belonging to the team.

# VI

# In Freedom's Chains

THE NEW ERA held the promise that blacks would work within the system, rather than agitate from without, that the reunited nation would be able to enforce a standard for human rights throughout the land. They expected the government to be an instrument in the advancement of black people. A black leader could now hope to make Congress and the president allies in his cause. Douglass realized that it would be important for him to be in Washington most of the time. Rochester had been an ideal place for an abolitionist agitator, but in the new era the best platform from which to reach a national audience would be Washington, D.C.

Douglass rejected some of the avenues of leadership now open to blacks. Friends suggested that he move to the South and seek elective office to Congress or to the Senate. Many years later he recalled why he rejected that path: "The thought of going to live among a people in order to gain their vote and gain official honors was repugnant to my self-respect." He did not see himself as a politician; his style of oratory would not be "effective with the newly enfranchised classes." As he saw it, his Northern and New England training had unsuited him to the Southern stump. One who "could tear a passion to tatters" would have "far better success with the masses there than one so little boisterous" as he.

Early in 1866 Chief Justice Solmon P. Chase had suggested that Douglass establish a press in Virginia, which would serve the cause of the freedman and equal rights. In responding, Douglass expressed the belief that both the future of blacks and the nation as a whole would rest more on the "sentiments and opinions of the people of the North and West than upon those of the South." The power had shifted from the South, he thought, and he had "an audience readymade in the free states, one which the labors of thirty years had prepared me for."

Douglass had discovered, somewhat to his surprise, that he was much in demand on the lecture circuit. Now that slavery was ended, the nation and the future no longer threatened by it, Northern and Western audiences were eager to see and hear this former slave who had advised presidents and been a major force in bringing about the changes they were witnessing. He could command from $100 to $200 a lecture, and he was in enough demand to make a comfortable living from such appearances.

He expanded the topics on which he would lecture, taking on subjects far beyond race relations and civil rights. Among other things, he offered to speak on the Hittites, Galileo, Scandinavian history, and Icelandic sagas. Remarking on the variety of his lecture topics, Douglass was reminded of the old temperance reformer, John B. Gough, who said, " 'Whatever may be the title, my lecture is always Temperance.' " So it is, Douglass mused, "with any man who has devoted his time and thought to one subject." By far his most popular lecture was "Self-Made Men."

His lectures and his interests in Washington kept him away from home much of the time. All that kept him in Rochester was his house and his family, and that tie was severed on 2 June 1872 when his home burned in a fire thought to be of suspicious origins. No one in his family was injured, but he suffered a considerable financial loss. Most painful to him was the destruction of the files of the *North Star* and *Frederick Douglass' Paper*. As he was later to remark, his most important formative and creative period was between 1848 and 1865. The physical remains of that labor had been his journalism, and that would now survive only in the scattered issues of his papers others had managed to keep. Within a month of the fire Douglass packed up what was left and moved his family to Washington.

A year and a half before the fire he had purchased a Washington-based newspaper, the *New National Era.* He had been persuaded early in 1870 to become a corresponding editor for what was then called the *New Era.* Several black men, including J. Sella Martin and George T. Downing, had started the paper out of the conviction that blacks, especially freedmen, needed a new journal serving their interests. From the first, Douglass discouraged them from the project, doubting that it could raise sufficient capital to stay solvent for long. He was, nevertheless, drawn more and more into the enterprise. His son Lewis, who, because of the bias of white workers, had been unable to work as a printer, became the paper's chief compositor. Douglass was naturally interested in helping to further his son's career. Within a year, however, Douglass's prediction of financial troubles proved all too true, and he was forced to buy the paper to keep it alive. Acutely conscious, as always, of the effect the paper's failure would have on the image of blacks in "the eyes of our white countrymen and to the outside world," Douglass was loath to see it go under.

He would not, however, throw himself again into a career in journalism. He used his editorials in the *New National Era* to give voice to his opinions on Reconstruction, race relations, labor, and education. Yet, he did nothing to make the paper his personal mouthpiece, telling his readers that he did not necessarily subscribe to columns not under his byline. He was merely doing his part to keep a worthy enterprise afloat.

The Freedman's Savings and Trust Company was another institution, carrying the hopes and reputation of black people, that Douglass felt called upon to save.

In 1865 a group of private investors gained a federal charter for the freedman's bank, charged with helping the newly emancipated slave get an economic foothold by saving. The enterprise caught on among freedmen, many thinking wrongly that it was a governmental institution. They poured their savings into the bank. By 1872 there were thirty two branches in the Southern states whose total deposits exceeded three million dollars. Although it was not, in fact, a black-managed bank, it deliberately sought that image. The tellers and all conspicuous employees in the marbled and magnificent Washington offices were attractive young black men and women.

The trustees were either careless or indifferent in the management of the depositors' savings, and speculators were able to appropriate the bank's assets at extraordinarily favorable rates. The banker, Jay Cooke, for instance, borrowed $500,000 from the freedman's bank at five percent interest at the very moment his own vast enterprise was on the verge of collapse. The crash of Jay Cooke and Sons precipitated the national economic crisis of 1873 in which the freedman's bank was brought to its knees.

After several runs on the bank, which was suffering a deficit of over $200,000, the trustees offered Frederick Douglass the presidency of the bank, hoping that his name would inspire confidence among the black depositors and prevent further runs. The situation, however, was too far gone for such a solution to be effective. Douglass accepted the position, not knowing how bad matters were. He knew only what a bitter loss the bank's collapse would be to the freedmen who had invested their first earnings; and, as always, he was sensitive to the appearance of failure in the "eyes of our white countrymen."

Color prejudice had conditioned whites to expect little from blacks, and blacks to expect little from themselves. The race could ill afford, Douglass thought, failures on so grand a scale. While it was true that the trustees painted a rosy picture of the bank's condition, Douglass's own vanity served to obscure the obvious, and convinced him that his name and prestige could make the crucial difference in the bank's life or death.

He sent telegrams throughout the South trying to persuade depositors that the bank was sound and would pay dollar for dollar in a short time. Confidence was all that was needed. Backing up his words, Douglass deposited thousands of dollars of his own money. He was soon to discover, however, that things were quite hopeless. Many of the trustees had been for some time quietly withdrawing their own funds, hoping to cut their losses. In his view of responsibility, Douglass could not follow them and leave thousands of his people to bear the brunt alone.

On 20 June 1874 Douglass went to Congress and secured an act placing the freedman's bank in bankruptcy. Despite his hopes that reorganization could save it, the trustees voted to close the bank's doors on June 28. The depositors would wait many years to get any of their money back, and even then, they got less than fifty cents on the dollar. As late as 1890, Douglass was still helping claimants get some of their money back. In a letter to Gerrit Smith, he summed up the matter in a familiar sentiment: "It has been the black man's cow, but the white man's milk."

All in all, 1874 was a bad year for Douglass's efforts to keep up a good front for black enterprises. In September the *New National Era,* into which Douglass had poured $10,000, folded. His sons, Lewis and Frederick, Jr., had managed the paper through four years of struggle. That, as much as anything else, had motivated Douglass to continue putting money into an enterprise he knew from the beginning would have little chance of survival. As much as the image of black people suffered, Douglass himself sustained considerable loss in the failures of the freedman's bank and the *New National Era.*

During the first years following the war, Douglass seemed to want, more than anything else, to be appointed to public service. He studiously avoided the appearance of an office seeker. He had contempt for such people who were caricatures in the Washington scene. He was, nevertheless, very conscious that it was reasonable for a Republican administration—dependent as they were on black votes—to appoint black men to office. It was not that they should pander to black voters, but that they should show the party's commitment to a future of racial justice. The deliberate and careful appointment of a qualified black man to public office would go far in educating a public —long weaned on color prejudice—as to the competence of blacks as citizens and leaders. Douglass was not wrong in thinking that he was the most logical choice of black man for such an honor.

His personal life history had always been his strongest asset. Who he was, where he had come from, the road he traveled were never far from his conscious mind. A slave, he had found the spirit of freedom compelling, by dint of will and courage had grasped it and become renowned on two continents, had served in the liberation of his people and the transformation of a nation, had advised presidents. He was a breathtaking representation of the American dogma of human perfectibility.

Now, well into his fifties, he kept analyzing and reconsidering that life story and its meaning. It pleased him to discover touchstones verifying and objectifying that past. He went to considerable trouble to find Amanda Auld Sears, the daughter of his former mistress Lucretia Auld, and he was greatly pleased at the friendship and sympathy he could establish with the woman after so many years, now that they were adult. Such encounters served to calibrate the distance he and the nation had traveled, to sustain the notion that his had been a special calling.

He undoubtedly saw public service in these terms, as an honor to himself, of course, but also as a milestone for the race and the nation. Through such a position he could be of service to his people, not only by what he could do in office, but in how he deported himself while in the public eye. Although this was vanity of a kind, it was certainly human. Whatever he imagined he might achieve through public office, the trick was not to become an "office seeker," for that would be corrupting. He could not want office so much that he would compromise himself, but he had to hold himself available.

He had been disappointed in the past on this score, and he would be so again. His hopes for a military commission had been dashed when Secretary of War Stanton failed to fulfill his promise. Other black men, however, would be given such commissions. Martin R. Delany was given a Major's rank to carry out recruiting in South Carolina. He was later to serve as an officer in the Freedmen's Bureau and, in time, a functionary in Wade Hampton's Democratic government in South Carolina. Douglass aspired to more than that, but nothing was offered him.

Andrew Johnson's test of Douglass's willingness to replace General O. O. Howard as head of the Freedmen's Bureau had been tempting. It was just the kind of office he would have wanted: conspicuously important and powerful, where he would have a role in shaping the future of Southern race relations. If Johnson had indeed extended such an offer, however, it would have been impossible for him to accept it. Yet, it might not be too much to expect President Grant to give such a post to a black man, especially since black votes played an important role in his election.

Grant, however, had no intention of making a black man superior to a large staff of whites, nor was he willing to give a black man any position in his administration. Aside from the appointment to the Santo Domingo Commission, Douglass received no offers. His name was tossed about when Grant appointed a black man, Ebenezer D. Bassett, as minister to Haiti in 1870. J. Sella Martin thought Douglass should have been offered the post and pressed the issue through Senator Charles Sumner the president would not change his mind.

The confusion over Bassett's appointment revealed Douglass's eagerness and his dilemma. When Bassett's name came before the Senate in 1869, some of the senators complained that Douglass was the best man for the job. Several blacks in Washington, hoping to defend Bassett and prevent the post from falling out of black hands altogether, argued that Douglass had expressed disinterest because it would require of him a financial sacrifice and force him to leave the country. Douglass wrote a strong rebuke to George T. Downing for whatever role he had in spreading that false rumor.

He had been deprived of the right to say yes or no on his own behalf, he complained; and furthermore, he had been misrepresented. He wanted to set the matter straight with Downing, at least. Money would not have been an object with him. He had no aversion to leaving the country. He had been made to look silly, rejecting an offer that had never been made to him. The rumors, he feared, would make government officials reluctant to make him offers in the future. True, he had not been conspicuously looking for a government job. What Downing failed to see, he chided, was the "wide difference between desiring and seeking office on the one hand, and that even temper and disposition of mind on the other, which might lead a man to accept a post of honor, when . . . adjudged worthy to fill it, by those who are supposed to be capable of forming an intelligent judgment."

Concerned that the public not misunderstand him, he wrote his friend, Theodore Tilden, asking him to publish his version of the issue in the *Independent.* "It is quite true," Douglass wrote, "I never sought this office or any other, but it is equally true that I have never declined it, and it is also true that I would have accepted, had it been offered."

Knowing Douglass's mind, J. Sella Martin continued to press Charles Sumner to try and attain a ministry for him, perhaps in Brazil or Costa Rico. Sumner finally wrote Martin, expressing his view that it would be a mistake for Douglass, and a loss to the cause of equal rights, were he to take a post outside the United States. In any case, Grant made no offers.

Douglass took little notice of his nomination in 1872 as vice-presidential candidate on the Equal-Rights ticket, headed by Victoria C. Woodhull. Rather, he threw himself vigorously into the campaign to reelect Grant. The election was marked by a split in the Republican party, with liberal Republicans like Carl Schurz and Charles Sumner breaking away to support the candidacy of Horace Greeley. It was mainly through Douglass's efforts that large numbers of black voters did not follow Sumner. The importance of Douglass's labors to the reelection of Grant was widely acknowledged, and there was talk that he would be given a position in the cabinet. Still, Grant made no offers.

Douglass carefully avoided showing any sign of disappointment. His rather aristocratic notion that proper political style should be free of personal interest obliged him to bear his feelings of ingratitude and injustice without signs of resentment. He did not want to appear a sycophant, groveling for patronage. For an office to be an "honor," one must be deemed "worthy" by those "supposed capable of forming an intelligent judgment." One should merit office, not earn it by mere political service. With such views, it would be impossible for him to press his own claims to the president, and there seemed no one with influence willing to do it in his stead. So, he remained a willing, but frustrated, candidate throughout the Grant administration.

Douglass did manage to win appointments under the next two Republican presidents. Rutherford Hayes, in 1877, appointed him United States marshal for the District of Columbia, a largely ceremonial office which he was to resign four years later. President James Garfield wanted to give that office to someone else, so he asked for Douglass's resignation, appointing him instead to the post of recorder of deeds for the District of Columbia.

Ironically, both of these were the kind of patronage positions which ordinarily went to the very party hacks Douglass held in contempt. There was no power attached to these offices; no policy was made in them. They were, nevertheless, visible signs of personal achievement, they carried the prestige of office, paid well, and were secure for the life of the administration. Though they may have fallen short of his hopes and expectations, Douglass seemed pleased to have such appointments, making the most of whatever honor there was in them.

He was careful in the administration of his offices that not the slightest complaint be leveled at him for either corruption or racial favoritism in hiring. Although he had to settle for being a petty functionary and bureaucrat rather than a policy maker, he would be exemplary, nonetheless.

A decade as a Washington office holder, keeping himself available for the next and better appointment, cherishing a bit too much the honors that fell to him, cost something in the sharpness and power of his social and political critique. The wit and satire of his prewar rhetoric had depended on his willingness to attack the most sacred of cows in American life. Presidents, politicians, political parties, the church and its clergy had all suffered Douglass's relentless attack. As he had seen it, nothing but reason, truth, and behavior consistent with principle deserved respect.

In antebellum days his enemies were clear, easy targets, and distant from him. Slaveholders and their friends, the profiteers from slavery, those who were complacent to the evil and social poison of race prejudice, the moralistic, hypocritical clergymen and politicians were all easy to attack. In the 1870s he would still rail against the unchanged attitudes of Southern whites, the disloyal Democratic party and its conservative Republican allies, and those who continued to deny to blacks the respect due them as citizens. Republicans in power who determined reconstruction policy were ambiguous friends and, therefore elusive targets.

Republican presidents from Grant through Harrison deserved sharp criticism from Douglass, but he was always gentle and generous, granting them much higher motives than they deserved.

Douglass was certainly not ready to accept things as they were, but he was awestruck that the lot of Afro-Americans had changed so markedly right before his eyes. Although he would continue to demand better protection of the rights of black people, he was not as willing as he once was to question the system or the leadership under which such remarkable change had occurred. Being relatively close to presidents, and assuming himself influential with them, he became highly respectful of their office, as well as tolerant and deferential to them.

Circumstances were, in fact, different from what they had been before the war, and it was reasonable to expect that a new style and new tactics would be most effective. Previously, the official government view of Afro-Americans had been that of Chief Justice Taney: they were not citizens of the United States and had no rights a white man need respect. Now that there could be no doubt that blacks were citizens, everything depended on whether the government would be vigorous, half-hearted, or unfriendly in the enforcement of the new dictum. Something could be gained from the administrations of Grant, Hayes, and Garfield. However little it might be, the alternatives to these men were dismal, indeed. Criticism and attack on their administrations, although deserved, might well serve to undermine those who at least seemed friendly, helping to put in office those who would be hostile to political equality for Afro-Americans.

These considerations tended to soften Douglass's public statements about national policy. He never actually advocated anything less than full citizenship and justice for blacks, but he was unwilling to lay the blame for shortcomings at the feet of the Republican leadership. Age, too, probably had something to do with his mellowing. He was well into his sixties, and many of his old abolitionist friends had retired from the fray, feeling self-satisfaction in having led a triumphant fight. Like them, Douglass probably hoped to rest a bit on his laurels, to enjoy the fruits of his youthful labor, to avoid fights he lacked the energy or the years to see through to the end.

Some complained that Douglass was indulging himself too much in the glory of his past, was too comfortable and secure with his income from lecturing and political office. Although he continued to make public complaint about Jim Crow practices in hotels and restaurants, he was silent about the slights he suffered as a member of the Santo Domingo Commission.

He made public excuses for President Grant's failure to invite him to the White House with the rest of the commission, but in a private letter to Charles Sumner, he expressed some bitterness. Some blacks thought he should have made an issue of President Hayes's taking some ceremonial functions from the United States marshal during Douglass's tenure. Certainly, such things were too petty to worry about, but Douglass wrote a rather long public statement defending the president(and himself in accepting the office)with the obvious point that Hayes had the right to choose who would introduce foreign visitors to him.

In all of this Douglass's prose took on the voice of office. Whereas before he had been slashing and sarcastic, he was now clever and a bit pompous.

A more serious criticism was that by accepting office from President Hayes, he was sanctioning the new Republican program in the South, including the removing of remaining troops, which essentially meant the abandonment of Southern blacks to their former masters. Douglass could explain that he had not known, at first, what Hayes's policy would be. He had conferred with him early in February 1877, and been assured that his Southern policy would be satisfactory. Hayes promised, then, to defend the rights of freedmen in the South, but the compromise which settled the disputed Tilden-Hayes election would change things. Almost immediately after taking office under Hayes, as if to show that he was not gagged, Douglass gave an address in Baltimore in which he lashed out at Jim Crow practices in the nation's capital.

In a speech in Washington on 7 November 1877 Douglass let it be known that "office-holder though I am," President Hayes's way of bringing peace to the South "is not my may, nor do I believe it will or ought to succeed." He could still speak his mind, but there was a pathos even in that. Douglass's rationale for holding office was that he could be of influence in shaping policy, but he had to see that he could do nothing to prevent the abandonment of blacks by the Republican party.

Still highly respected by black Americans, Douglass's leadership in the 1870s and 1880s was nonetheless criticized by them. He would have liked to have been an elder statesman, but the circumstances of black Americans in the postwar decades did not permit that role. It must be said that none of the black leaders from the antebellum years were more aggressive or radical than Douglass during the trying time of Reconstruction. Some, like Martin Delany, ended up serving the interests of a conservative Southern government. Neither was there a younger generation of black leadership to apply radical pressure which might have made Douglass's moderation more effective. It would be another fifty years before a black man of national stature would emerge who would be aggressive and assertive about the rights of black people.

It was only common sense that blacks should find the political party that best served their interests, and support it with their work and loyalty. Most black leaders, including Douglass, logically chose the Republican party; the Democratic party was unthinkable. The facts of postwar politics, however, forced them to ask "which Republican party," so fractious was it then. Here, too, the choices open to them were far from ideal.

Douglass had shared in creating certain myths on which postwar politics was to thrive. He had been among the first to imbue the martyred Lincoln with the spirit of the Great Emancipator, and to dub the Republicans as the party of freedom. The radical Republicans, who had little respect for the living Lincoln, were ready to join Northerners and Southern blacks in his apotheosis in death. It served them to do that, as it had served them to take up the championship of the freedman in their fight to unseat Andrew Johnson. It would have been impossible to separate the false from the genuine among them.

Douglass seemed to forget the unpromising origins of the Republican party, how far it had always been from abolitionism. He seemed not to remember the pain and soul-searching it had caused him to support the party in 1856 and 1860. He similarly repressed under the sentiment of martyrdom his bitter disappointment with Lincoln's slow and grudging acceptance of the inevitability of emancipation and the use of black troops. Douglass had once written of Lincoln that he does *"evil by choice, right by necessity,"* but that was lost in the postwar glow of triumph. He had said, from the beginning, that the war was revolutionary and would master events and presidents. Men may have wanted to contain it, to fight it with limited liabilities, but they would be transformed despite themselves into abolitionists. Events seemed to prove him a prophet, were providential; it was as if God's hand had guided them all along, beyond their wills, beyond their imaginations, beyond their capacities. His mistake was to hope that the momentum had actually transformed the men and the party.

Douglass's continued faith in the Republican party and its leadership was a faith not so much in the men and the institution but in history. The events of history made things happen and forced men to accommodate themselves. The party had to ally itself to the freedman, he thought, if it hoped to continue to function as a national party. It was in the party's interest to protect the freedman in his newly won rights. In the short run, the freedman might be manipulated, but with experience he would direct his influence in constructive ways to build a free society. As the American society had been caught up in the winds of change, propelled closer to its true destiny of liberty and humanity, the momentum would carry them even further to the completion of the transformation. That would be the achievement of the revolution, and the Republican party, for its own survival, would have to be an instrument in making it come to pass.

It was, perhaps, a naive faith. While some Republicans went so far as to imagine a new South ruled by an alliance of friendly

Southern whites, Northern white migrants, and black voters, none were prepared to replace the traditional Southern leadership in the South with blacks. So the radical Republicans' program was fraught with contradictions.

They supported radical Reconstruction for a variety of reasons. Some, noting the return of old-line Southern leadership to power and to Congress under Andrew Johnson, were anxious to delay their influence on national policy. During the war, with the South out of the Union, Congress had been able to pass high tariff schedules, establish a national banking system, and adopt a liberal land policy in the Homestead Act. National policy had been tailored to the interests of the Northeast and the West, free from Southern opposition. An early return of Southerners to power would likely jeopardize these programs. Others keenly aware that the Republican party had been a minority, sectional party before the war, were anxious to find ways of broadening the party's base. It was to be feared that the agricultural West might find common cause with the new South and establish a sectional alliance which would reduce the power of the industrial Northeast.

They needed to find Republican strength in the South. There were some, like Lincoln, who had hoped that strength would come from former Southern Whigs and Unionists, but in time that would be coupled with a reliance on black voters.

A few Republicans took the idea of a "Southern rebellion" very much to heart, holding that the "slave power" and the Confederate leadership had been guilty of treason and should be punished. They wanted to impose a harsh policy on the culprits, depriving them of political power and property. It was not that they cared so much for the freedman, but because they shared the sentiment expressed by Andrew Johnson: "Treason must be made infamous and traitors must be impoverished."

There were, at last, a very few Republicans like Charles Sumner and John Hale, who were genuinely concerned that justice be given to blacks. That meant that they should be made free, given political power, and protected in their rights.

This coalition was fragile enough. It had been able to unseat Johnson, establish congressional control over Reconstruction, and push through legislation and constitutional amendments giving freedmen some semblance of political rights. Beyond that, however, there was little to make it cohere.

The first fissures were to come early. Charles Sumner, out of personal dislike of President Grant, spurred by disagreements over Santo Domingo annexation and the early signs of corruption and shoddy administration, led a "liberal" break with the party in 1872. It was a strange alliance, which included Carl Schurz (then Senator from Missouri), Gideon Welles, Charles Francis Adams, and Horace Greeley. All of them were revolted by what they considered incompetence within the Grant administration and its growing corruption, but some advocated a moderation in the treatment of the South. They nominated Horace Greeley for president to oppose Grant, and the Democrats quickly nominated Greeley as well.

No white man of national stature could have challenged Charles Sumner as champion and advocate of black men's rights. The Democrats hoped he would draw sufficient black votes away from Grant to elect the Greeley ticket. Douglass and other black leaders worked tirelessly to hold black voters to Grant. It was painful for him to campaign against Sumner, but he correctly perceived that a party under the leadership of Gideon Welles, never a friend of black people, Carl Schurz and Horace Greeley, who were both erratic on race and preoccupied with civil service reform, would be a disaster for the freedman. They had to support Grant out of fear of alternatives.

Sumner remained, apart from his connection with the "independents," the strongest political champion of the freedman in Washington. He pushed through Congress a Civil Rights Bill in March 1875. That bill, assuming the Fourteenth Amendment granted Congress power to legislate against private as well as state discrimination, guaranteed equal rights in public places without distinction of color and it forbade the exclusion of blacks from jury duty. But the government proved powerless, or lacking in will, to protect the rights of blacks in the South.

Combining violence, coercion, and fraud, blacks were being removed from what power they had. The series of "force bills," aimed at punishing as insurrectionary the organized violence against blacks, was partially successful in suppressing the Ku Klux Klan. But intimidation and violence by conservatives, and ambivalence by white Republicans, continued to have a deadening effect on Southern black political freedom. Conservative Democratic governments began returning to power in Southern states. By 1871 Georgia, North Carolina, Tennessee, and Virginia had been lost. Alabama, Arkansas, Mississippi, and Texas followed by 1875. By the Tilden-Hayes compromise, removing the remaining federal troops from the South and, in effect, abandoning efforts to enforce the "force bills," only Florida, Louisiana, and South Carolina remained in radical hands; the rest of the South had been lost to the Democrats.

Republicans continued far into the 1880s to run against the wartime activities of the Democratic party. They assumed to themselves the mantle of national loyalty and attempted to paint their Democratic opponents as dishonorable traitors. They would, at times, employ the antislavery rhetoric which gave to them and their party the role of liberators, and named the Democrats heirs to the "slaveocracy." This "waving the bloody shirt," as it was called, served to avoid difficult issues such as the tariff, money policy, and corruption. It hardly spoke of a continued commitment to wartime ideals. Most Republicans, once they were assured of their party's viability and of the permanence of wartime economic measures, were quite content that blacks be "removed from politics" altogether.

Douglass and other black leaders naturally saw matters in a

different light. From the end of the war on, the old Southern leadership, through the Democratic party, was attempting to return as close as possible to the way things had been. That meant their return to power and blacks to servility, minimizing as much as possible the effects of the postwar amendments. This could be accomplished outside the law by lynchings, murders, economic pressure, and intimidation. As Douglass saw it, the Democratic party was attempting to erase the achievements of the war.

So Douglass, in his editorials and speeches, adopted the same language as other Republicans, but with a difference. He believed that the paramount issue of the postwar years was the securing of the rights of the freedman. That came before tariffs, banking, or civil service reform. Rather than "waving the bloody shirt," Douglass was trying to maintain focus on the enemy of true national unity—to hold Republicans to the principles of liberty and freedom their rhetoric echoed, to the ideals over which he insisted the war had been fought. At every turn, however, he was to be reminded that these principles had never run very deep with Republicans, or the white American public either.

These were frustrating years for all black leaders. Martin Delany, now in South Carolina, had seen radical Reconstruction at work. He wrote to the *New National Era* in August 1871 expressing his disillusionment and disgust. Although he was an immigrant from the North himself, he complained of white carpetbaggers and their manipulation of the politically naive freedman. He was discouraged with the freedman's ignorance of politics, his susceptibility to manipulation and corruption. He denounced black men for going armed to political meetings. He complained of the insolence and bad manners of many freedmen. These were strange remarks from a black man whose antebellum reputation was of radicalism beyond that of Douglass.

Douglass patiently answered Delany in the columns of the *New National Era.* Carpetbaggers posed problems, many were corrupt, but many others were selfless and highly motivated. It was foolish to have expected black men to come out of slavery as sophisticated political beings. True, they had allowed themselves to become the "backs and legs upon which white men ride to power," but laboring classes were so used everywhere. It would take time. Going armed into Southern political meetings made good sense to Douglass; blacks had not started the practice, but they needed to protect themselves. "I shall never ask the colored people to be lambs," he wrote, "where the whites insist on being wolves." He was shocked to read Delany's complaints about the freedmen's insolence of manners. Certainly that was to be preferred to the old signs of obedience and servitude. Delany's disillusionment grew more profound, however. He proceeded along a path that would give him office as a Democratic functionary under Wade Hampton in South Carolina.

Some blacks, like George T. Downing, grew restive because the payoff in black support of the Republican party was far from commensurate to the power they gave the party. Grant had been elected by black votes, and they constituted a crucial political balance. But neither in terms of appointments to office or policy was such loyalty repaid. Downing was not the first black man, nor would he be the last, who would suggest that black voters show real evidence that their support could not be taken for granted. In a letter to the *New National Era* in June 1871 he suggested that blacks split between the Republicans and the Democrats. That way, Republicans would have to work for their votes, giving more for them, and the Democrats, seeing the possibility of winning black support might become more liberal in their program. As long as blacks were only Republicans, Downing argued, neither party had the incentive to earn their support.

Douglass's answer was sharp. Such a policy as Downing suggested would be a disaster. If "we are slighted by the Republican party, we are murdered by the Democratic party." The Republican party "had within it the only element of friendship for the colored man's rights . . . it has done for us all that has been done in the past." To turn from it to the Democratic party for some calculated future benefit would be unthinkable.

The fact was, as Douglass's exchange with Downing revealed, there was no place for black votes to go. Because that was true, the Republicans could depend on them without fear of losing them to rivals. This meant that the power of the black vote could be used to save others while blacks remained supplicants, necessarily grateful for whatever their only friends were willing to give. It was a problem that would plague the Afro-American politician for a century to come. As the Republican party's internal strife continued, the choices for black leaders became even slimmer. The party's divisions, more over personalities than principles, had little directly to do with the right of blacks. The "Stalwarts," under Roscoe Conklin, would hold to the line on tariffs and would resist civil service reform. The "Half-breeds," under James G. Blaine, would be open to some reform on these issues. The independents, who had supported Greeley in 1872, now under the leadership of E. L. Godkin of the *Nation,* Carl Schurz, Charles Francis Adams, Jr., and George William Curtis, would place civil service reform above party loyalty. These "Mugwumps," as they were called, would help elect Grover Cleveland, the first postwar Democratic president in 1884.

Douglass's only choice was to adhere closely to the line of party orthodoxy. He would support the Stalwarts and Conklin without alienating Blaine and his followers. The Mugwumps, of course, were out of the question: their "independence" made them de facto Democrats. Most of them had an indifferent if not hostile attitude toward black Southern voters. Watching the displacement of old-line leadership in eastern cities by corrupt political machines empowered by mass, illiterate immigrant voters, they discovered a new respect for the "natural leadership" of the South. The black man's political options were narrow, indeed.

Douglass had been astute in insisting, from the first talk of emancipation, that freedom was meaningless without political power. His own experience in the postwar years was to underline the truth of that in a special way. His entire life had been in the quest of freedom, his own and that of his people. During the antebellum years his alienation as a black man and radical allowed him the freedom of mind and spirit he would never have again. After the war, he became free as a man and citizen, he was allowed to belong to a nation. But, to paraphrase Chief Justice Taney, he had no *power* white men need respect. So, unless he was willing to break free from the system, to alienate himself again and speak from the outside, he would have to become the servant of the political choice, to learn the "art of the possible." For an Afro-American in the late nineteenth century, that was a fettered and confining freedom, indeed.

# VII
# The Declension

WITH DOUGLASS'S MOVE to Washington, the story of his life took on even more popular appeal; it became one of the greatest success stories of the era. The 1855 version of his autobiography continued to sell; and he would revise it again in 1881. Nearly ten years in government office gave him a financial security he had never before known. In 1878 he purchased a fifteen-acre estate with a twenty-room Victorian house just across the Anacostia branch of the Potomac River. "Cedar Hill," situated high above the Anacostia flats and overlooking Washington, D. C., symbolized his ascendance.

Ironically, the condition of blacks, particularly in the South, was deteriorating in these same years. The Democratic recapture of state governments in the South, the steady withdrawal of federal troops, violence, and economic pressure by whites conspired to push blacks out of politics. The gradual, de facto disenfranchisement of blacks, beginning in the 1870s, was to be codified in "grandfather clauses" and other legal devices by the end of the century.

By 1900 Douglass's dream of a Southern black political weight would be dead, though it would take considerable violence and bloodshed to deprive Southern blacks of the rights they seemed to have won in the wartime amendments. Gone, too, would be the dreams of economic independence for the black farmer. The freedmen's expectations of land would go unfulfilled, and they would be obliged to return to labor for former slaveholders on terms the white men set. The tenant and sharecropping system would throw them into chronic indebtedness so that they would owe their labor in advance, making their lot hardly better than that of slaves. They would retain few advantages of freedom, none of power. Still they would be obliged, as freemen, to provide their own food, clothing, and shelter.

With the old antislavery force dead or dying, there were few to bring down moral censure on an indifferent public or the nation's leaders. New England liberals, facing their own political ordeal with democracy as immigrant-supported political machines displaced them from power, were revolted by the disorder and corruption they saw in reconstruction governments. They were anxious to return all government to the hands of the "natural leadership." Charles Sumner died in 1874, leaving his Civil Rights Bill as the monument of his commitment to the cause of black Americans. It would be the last such legislation for a century.

At least Douglass had been right. If the old order was allowed to return to power, without some guarantees and protection to freedmen, the whites would bend every effort to beat blacks back into a place of dependency and powerlessness. If they could not have slaves, they would have peons. His critics would complain, however, that Douglass had become too removed from poor blacks, too complacent and self-satisfied to see the process properly and hold his Republican friends accountable for their duplicity.

There was some justice to the criticism that Douglass had grown away from the real plight of Southern blacks. This was nowhere more apparent than in his failure to grasp the full significance of growing number of blacks who wanted to migrate from the South.

By 1880 thousands of Southern blacks had begun a movement from the deep South into Kansas, Missouri, and Indiana. "Pap" Singleton led the "exodusters" into Kansas. Some, like Richard T. Greener, Dean of the Howard University Law

School, would argue that migration from the South would benefit not only those who left, giving them a chance to start again outside the region of their former degradation, but that even those remaining stood to gain as whites' dependency on their labor became more apparent and wages rose.

Douglass viewed these movements much as he had the antebellum emigrationist schemes. He insisted that to migrate was simply to give up the fight in the South and acquiesce in the national government's unwillingness to fulfill its obligations. The black man's power rested on two facts: he constituted the labor on which the South depended to rebuild, and his citizenship rights had been established in the Constitution. He must stay put, exploit the one, and defend the other.

Indeed these migrants were harassed by Southern whites who, however much they despised the blacks, were anxious lest their cheap labor vanish. Those who managed to leave got rough welcomes in prospective homes where whites had no intention of encouraging an influx of Southern blacks. The migration fizzled, though its failure was of little comfort of Douglass.

The Supreme Court further shattered Douglass's faith that the revolution securing citizenship rights for blacks had been sealed in the Constitution. He had imagined, along with the framers of the Fourteenth Amendment, that the intent and effect of the amendment was to modify federalism so that the national government would guarantee civil rights to all citizens. Before the war, the government had been powerless to reach within the states to prevent the tyrannical oppression of slavery. The amendment corrected that and, as Douglass saw it, the national government needed only the will to do what it had been empowered to do. Two decisions of the Supreme Court, a decade apart, ended that illusion.

In the *Slaughterhouse* cases of 1873 the Supreme Court, speaking through Justice Samuel F. Miller, refused to construe the privilege-and-immunities clause of the Fourteenth Amendment as having done away with the distinction between state and national citizenship, that conceit used by Roger Taney in the *Dred Scott* decision to deny blacks status as citizens before the Court. Douglass, along with others, had supposed that the Fourteenth Amendment's assertion that "All persons born or naturalized in the United States . . . are citizens of the United States and of the States wherein they reside" had settled that matter against Taney's interpretation.

While the *Slaughterhouse* cases had not been brought as a matter pertaining to the rights of black people, the decision had devastating implications for their hopes. Understanding clearly the meaning of Justice Miller's decision, Douglass condemned it in a letter to Gerrit Smith. "Two citizenships means no citizenship," he wrote. "The true doctrine is one nation, one citizenship, and one law for all the people." Still, Douglass made no public issue of it.

The Supreme Court decision in the *Civil Rights* cases a decade later, however, could not be taken calmly. It struck down Charles Sumner's Civil Rights Act of 1875, which had made it a misdemeanor to deny any person equal rights and privileges in inns, theaters and places of amusement, and public transportation. The act had imposed federal sanctions against practices of racial discrimination Northern free blacks had always been subjected to and which had become prevalent in the postwar South.

Writing for the Court, Justice Joseph P. Bradley denied that the amendment empowered Congress to legislate except against state action. "Individual invasion of individual rights is not the subject matter of the amendment," he wrote. Thus Congress would have to wait for states to pass offensive legislation before it could countermand it. It could place no sanctions on individual behavior which had no specific state authorization.

The Court's decision was shocking to those who had assumed that the Civil War amendments affected fundamental change in national power to govern race relations. At a mass meeting in Washington on 22 October 1883 Frederick Douglass was among the principal speakers protesting the Court's action.

Douglass, however, was guarded. He was, after all, recorder of deeds for the District of Columbia. He presumed his words carried the weight of office, and his tone was cautious and a bit officious. Not to be misrepresented or distorted, he had taken the unusual precaution of writing out his remarks in full.

He well understood the passion aroused by the Court's decision, recalling the old Fugitive Slave Act and the *Dred Scott* decision. Yet he had not come to attack and condemn. As he saw it, among the great evils threatening "our free institutions" was the "increasing want of respect" for those who govern. "We should never forget," he declared, "that, whatever may be the incidental mistakes and misconduct of rulers, government is better than anarchy, and patient reform is better than violent revolution." He hoped his remarks would disappoint anyone expecting from him a "violent denunciation of the Supreme Court." Responsible criticism, nevertheless, was in order. Free speech and civic responsibility demanded no less.

Douglass was forced to admit that the Civil Rights Act of 1875 had become, in effect a "dead letter," so poorly was it enforced. That in no way mitigated, however, the devastating effect of the Court declaration that the legislation was unconstitutional. It had been "advanced legislation . . . a banner on the outer wall of American liberty, a noble moral standard, uplifted for the education of the American people." Enforced or not, the act spoke of justice and fair play: "It told the American people that they were all equal before the law; that they belonged to a common country and were equal citizens." The Supreme Court had pulled that banner down. Its decision, he declared, "is a concession to race pride, selfishness, and meanness, and will be received with joy by every upholder of caste in the land, and for this I deplore and denounce that decision."

Still, he was careful so as not to be misunderstood. "I utterly deny," he took pains to say, "that there has ever been any denunciation of the Supreme Court on this platform, and I defy any man to point out one sentence or syllable of any speech of mine in denunciation of that Court." Such was the burden of office.

Being settled in Washington afforded Douglass, for the first time in his life, the chance to enjoy his family. He was reasonably secure, financially, and he no longer had to travel constantly, filling lecture dates as a livelihood. His home gave him more space and comfort than he had ever known. It was much too late, however, to change well-established patterns and create what had not been nurtured from the beginning.

Douglass's heart, after all, had never been at the hearthside. He had thrived in the public arena. If anything, home and family served as a temporary retreat from forays into a hostile and contentious world. Even so, family had served his public image. In typically nineteenth-century style, Douglass was anxious to project the image of the happy family man, yet not intrude private and personal matters into public debate.

He had, of course, shown fatherly pride with all his children, and a reader of his paper could not but know it. He made a public issue of Rosetta's being barred on racial grounds from admission to the Rochester public schools. He had also brought to the public's attention the enlistments of Charles and Lewis in the Massachusetts' 54th Regiment. Aside from such comment his public utterances and even his private letters and autobiographies are remarkably free of any references to his wife and children or his feelings and anxieties about them.

Certainly he was a warm, affectionate, and proud father. He enjoyed playing the violin and singing for his children when he was at home. He took pride in their accomplishments and doubtless reflected often on the difference between his own childhood and theirs; much of their advantage was due to his own exertion and personal triumph. They reflected Douglass's own courage, talent, and celebrity. His children would be able to claim little pride in their own right, however.

Douglass might have wondered, as do many self-made men, at the irony of it all: his children had many of the advantages he could only dream of as a slave, yet their accomplishments were rather slight. Rosetta married a man who had himself been a fugitive slave; Nathan Sprague, however, turned out to be an alcoholic and ne'er-do-well, and their family remained dependent on Douglass. Lewis and Frederick, Jr. had great difficulty establishing themselves. Both had experience in journalism and would follow in their father's path. Never, however, would they act as independent men; they relied, instead, on their father's success and reputation. Douglass helped all he could, perhaps encouraging their dependence on him. He poured over ten thousand dollars into his sons' publishing venture, which came to a total loss for them all. He continued to indulge his children and grandchildren throughout his life, but he had been unable to give them that hunger for personal freedom and independence which had so much shaped his own life.

In August 1882 Anna Murray Douglass died, ending a marriage of forty-four years. She had always been helpful to Douglass, in her reserved and domestic way. Encouraging him to escape, she had given him her life's savings to take with him. She had done domestic work to help support the family, taking time out to bear the children. It had been Anna Douglass's shrewd household management and frugality that allowed them to accumulate money; by the time of their move to Rochester they enjoyed reasonable comfort with the money Douglass could bring in from his lectures and the sale of his books. Through all the years Frederick spent traveling, it was Anna who saw that he was met by parcels of fresh linen at stops along the way. She took pride in her skills as a housekeeper and homemaker. Frederick could be sure that when he was away —whether for twenty months abroad or mere weeks on domestic tour—that Anna could take care of herself and the home. She, who had been born to free black parents in Maryland and trained to serve white people, lived to be mistress of Cedar Hill in Anacostia.

Nevertheless, it could hardly have been called a satisfying marriage. Frederick's ambitions and achievements pulled them into a world Anna had little wish to be part of. Eight years his senior and freeborn, she remained illiterate despite all his efforts to find teachers for her. That fact alone kept her out of the world of reform in which he moved. She was not comfortable in the presence of white people, and while their home in Rochester was the stopping place for all the major figures in abolition, temperance, and women's rights, Anna played the role of housekeeper and cook, seeing that they were comfortable and well-fed, and then retiring to leave them to talk with her husband. Though she may have respected Frederick for his accomplishments, she could not contribute to his intellectual and professional growth.

Frederick Douglass, however, was never without women friends who could serve his mind and ego as Anna could not. Physically an imposing man—over six feet tall, with leonine head and powerful voice—self-confident, brilliant, and of ready wit, he moved easily among whites as well as blacks. Women were always attracted to him, and many white women in the reform movement willingly defied racial etiquette to be seen with him. English women, in particular, showered him with so much public attention that his abolitionist friends feared lest he compromise himself.

Douglass enjoyed the attention, never doing anything to discourage it. Some of his closest friends would be English and American white women. He thrived on these friendships, not merely because they engaged him in the central reform issues of the day, but because they touched the very nerve of American racial prejudice. He knew very well that the most frightening bugbear to white Americans was the spector of black-male–white-female sexuality. The unflinching public display of such warm friendships were as a standard at the frontier of the racial struggle in America.

That is why Douglass took special delight in being seen in the company of white women. When his English friends, Eliza and Julia Griffiths, came to America, they made a point of being seen together on the streets of New York City, walking arm-in-arm in Rochester, traveling together on the overnight Hudson River steamer to Albany. Defying Jim Crow practices —forcing whites to eject him from trains, restaurants, and theaters—he willingly took the verbal abuse that public display of these friendships provoked. Often enough, he took and gave blows for his troubles.

To Frederick, Anna undoubtedly suffered in comparison to other women such as Julia Griffiths; clever, literate, and aggressive. Julia tutored him and was his confidante, helping him through the ideological thickets of Garrisonian and anti-Garrisonian abolition. In the two years Julia stayed in the Douglass home, he became more and more dependent on her. That did not please Anna, and Julia wrote Gerrit Smith of the "tensions" in the Douglass household. There was truth, then, to the rumors Garrison voiced in the *Liberator* about Julia being the cause of domestic discord. Still, Douglass, conscious of his image, never left himself open to charges of infidelity. He knew only too well that his single best resource was an unblemished, exemplary character.

Nevertheless, the shadow of Julia Griffiths hung over the Douglass household through the remainder of Anna's life. Although Julia married a Reverend H. O. Crofts some four years after her return to England, her correspondence with Douglass continued uninterrupted to the end of his life. It was not that Julia was an actual rival, but it was what she represented that haunted Frederick's and Anna's relationship. She was the kind of companion that Frederick wanted and needed but that Anna could not or would not become. There was no open hostility or bickering in their marriage; indeed it showed all the signs of rectitude and forbearance expected from the nineteenth-century American family. It seemed, however, to lack the full warmth and sense of companionship that they and their children might have desired.

It is not surprising, then, that a year and a half after Anna's death, Frederick remarried. While anyone might have predicted that his new wife would be white, it was nevertheless a shock and a sensation all around. A Rochester woman, educated at Mt. Holyoke Female Seminary, Helen Pitts met Douglass in Washington. She had been a secretary in the office of the recorder of deeds. She was forty-six when they married, and Douglass was sixty-six.

The news of their marriage was greeted with general hostility. Helen's family did the expected thing and disassociated themselves from her. The Douglass children, dependent as they were on their father, could not go that far but were not shy in expressing their strong disapproval. They continued, as was their habit, to come and go at Cedar Hill, but they were never friendly to Helen nor more than perfunctory in acknowledging her presence. The white press was predictably outraged, but blacks were no less offended. Some held that Douglass's act implied that no black woman was good enough for him; his act undermined arguments for equal rights by giving credence to the claim that a black man's highest aspiration was to have a white wife. Some complained that Helen was too ordinary, having neither money, nor class, nor status. To some, she was merely a clever woman who had hooked an old fool, expecting to inherit his money.

There were, on the other hand, whites and blacks who congratulated the couple. Reverend Francis J. Grimké, the black reformer and recognized kin of the white abolitionists, Angela and Julia Grimké, performed the ceremony and blessed the couple. Elizabeth Cady Stanton sent her best wishes as did Julia Griffiths Croft. Some blacks expressed their pleasure, seeing the marriage as a way of destroying the hypocrisy which accepted only those interracial unions that were not blessed by wedlock.

For his part Douglass seemed to enjoy the sensation his marriage caused. He found clever ways of explaining himself. He liked to say that he had proved himself impartial to race: his first wife "was the color of my mother, and the second, the color of my father." More to the point, his marriage to Helen Pitts exemplified the beliefs for which he stood. He had always rejected racial distinctions as unnatural and irrational. The fact that white and black Americans had found sexual partners in one another was everywhere to be seen. To have refused to do what he and Helen did, merely because of racial prejudice, would have sent him to his grave "a self-accused and a self-convicted moral coward."

His union with Helen Pitts, therefore, was another strike for freedom in which he broke free from the conventions of racial prejudice. No less was it a strike for independence from the constraints that black people themselves would place him under in the name of racial loyalty, demanding that he submerge his personal vision and individual desires to the interests of the race as seen by them. In this, too, he would follow his own path.

Although there had been general public criticism, Helen and Frederick suffered very little as a result of it. They seemed to have been very happy. He had in her a companion to take with him to meetings on women's rights as well as to literary societies where he enjoyed doing dramatic readings. They shared a musical interest and often spent their evenings playing: Helen at the piano and Frederick with his violin. Frederick was proud of Helen and liked being with her in public. Invitations to political and social receptions in Washington did not slacken, and he attended them with Helen always on his arm. When they returned home—the two of them riding in their carriage through the lily-white, middle-class Anacostia flats, up the steep rise to Cedar Hill and its white, Victorian house—there was a dramatic message in that, also. From that commanding height, the former slave could look down on Washington, the sordidness of politics and prejudice, and reflect on the transcendence of the indomitable human spirit.

In 1884 Grover Cleveland became the first Democratic president since James Buchanan and since the Civil War. Whatever else that meant, Douglass could expect to be asked to give up his office as the recorder of deeds. Cleveland, however, allowed him to remain in office for over a year before he asked for his resignation. Then, in September 1886, he and Helen embarked on an extensive tour of Europe. They visited England and Helen met Julia Griffiths Croft, Frederick and his old friend seeing one another for the first time in over twenty years. The Douglasses took the grand tour of the continent, and visited Egypt and Greece, returning to Washington after a full year abroad.

At home and no longer obliged by office or by loyalty to an administration, Douglass threw himself into the political swim. In March 1888 he traveled to South Carolina and Georgia and was deeply shaken by the deteriorating condition of black sharecroppers there.

In April he was invited to speak at the convention of the Woman's Suffrage Association and had a chance to recall the forty-six years of his involvement in that movement, from its first meetings in Seneca Falls. The bitterness over the Fifteenth Amendment and the struggle for black male suffrage had been forgotten. He shared the platform with Elizabeth Cady Stanton and Susan B. Anthony as in the old days.

1888 was an election year and Douglass hit the campaign trail. Despite his seventy-one years he campaigned vigorously for Benjamin Harrison in Connecticut, New York, New Jersey, Michigan, Indiana, and Iowa. It is not certain whether or not Douglass was working for a new appointment. His age certainly would not have kept him from taking on the light duties of such patronage posts as he had previously held. Political job or not, he continued to associate the future well-being of blacks in the South to Republican administrations. While he had become very disillusioned with Republicans in general, he felt that Democrats were worse. He laid much of the blame for the disheartening conditions of black sharecroppers in South Carolina and Georgia on the Democratic administration. It was not Cleveland himself, but the crowd of racially reactionary Democrats who were necessarily swept into office with the Democratic victory. Four years had been more than enough. It was time to bring Republicans back to office and oblige them to honor their promises.

When Harrison took office in 1889 he offered Douglass an appointment as minister-resident and consul-general to the Republic of Haiti. It was a curious offer, since Douglass no longer had the vigor to adapt readily to a tropical climate, and Haiti was far removed from the public forums he enjoyed. At seventy-one years old he had reason to suspect that in accepting the post, he might not live to see his native land again. Perhaps the offer was made knowing it was unlikely that he would accept it.

Harrison's offer stirred up considerable criticism in the press. Some New York papers complained that Douglass had no experience as a diplomat; that he was the wrong color since it was thought that the Haitians would prefer and respect a white man more; and that they would consider it as an insult that the United States government send a black man as minister. Furthermore, it was implied that any black American, his loyalty divided between race and nation, would have difficulty serving the interests of the United States in a black republic.

It was a strange furor. The appointment of Douglass was no new departure. Experience was seldom a consideration in foreign service appointments at that time. So tendentious was the criticism that Douglass was probably right in his reflection that it represented business interests' anxiety lest a black minister, especially Douglass, be an unwilling instrument in the American exploitation of Haiti. Douglass remarked that Naval officers were especially eager to feed the American press with information and innuendos which could be used against his appointment.

Even more curious than President Harrison's offer and the ensuing public clamor was Douglass's acceptance of the post. He had little to gain. It was going to be a difficult assignment, enervating even to a younger man, and breaking no new ground for blacks. For a man who enjoyed contemplating his achievements, this was not such a glorious accomplishment at all.

Perhaps it was hunger for achievement, the challenge he felt in the assignment, or despair over the deteriorating condition of blacks at home. Whatever his reasons for accepting the offer, he went—against the advice of most of his friends, who told him the office was "too small" for him, and that it was too risky for him to go to Haiti at his advanced age. They tried to remind him of the need for his voice in Washington. Julia Griffiths Croft wrote from England advising against acceptance. As she saw it the government was becoming troubled by the tone of his recent addresses "and they are politely sending you away, to a far country and leaving the poor coloured people of the U.S. *deprived* of their greatest & *truest* friend." She could see through it, however. "Oh! I do so fear and feel that you are leaving one important sphere of labor for another less important *& far more dangerous.*" Douglass took the post nonetheless, and he and Helen departed Washington late in September 1889.

His was a troubled mission from the start. Unable to obtain first-class rail or ship accommodations south, the Douglasses had to sail by naval vessel. The captain refused to eat at the same table with the black man and his wife, but Douglass insisted that he be treated the same as a white diplomat. The Douglasses took their meals in the officer's mess while the captain pridefully ate in his quarters.

Douglass arrived at Port-au-Prince on October 8, but his appointment was not confirmed by the Senate until December

17, delaying for two months his formal reception by the Haitian government. The American press, continuing to express its disapproval of Douglass, took this delay as a sign that the Haitian government was snubbing the black emissary. This was not at all the case. The Haitian people and government held Douglass in high esteem. Their warm reception, the continuous deference and respect paid to him, was probably the only positive thing he would bring away from this arduous and embarrassing service to his country.

Given the way the announcement of his appointment had been received at home, he could only expect carping and critical comment about his every act. He was serving the United States government and, as consul-general, American business interests at a time of feverish expansionism in the Caribbean. James G. Blaine, as Secretary of State, hoped to extend United States influence and power in Latin America and supported expansion in the Pacific with the annexation of the Hawaiian Islands. The U.S. Navy itself was beginning to develop a global vision, amplifying the teachings of Alfred Thayer Mahan, whose *The Influence of Sea Power in History* shaped their thinking from its publication in 1890. Douglass could hardly have been comfortable as an agent of this strategy, identifying as he did with black people and idealizing the revolutionary tradition of Haiti. Because of his race consciousness, he would be unable automatically to share kinship with the white American businessmen and naval officers who saw Haiti as a plum for profit and power.

Douglass had no problem accepting an expansionist American policy in the Caribbean. He had supported, in 1871, President Grant's efforts to annex Santo Domingo. He genuinely believed that the island and its people would benefit as a territory of the United States and was convinced that the Dominicans wanted annexation. Similarly, during his ministry, he believed that Haitians and Dominicans would gain from increased trade with the United States. He saw nothing wrong with expecting the Haitians to make trade attractive and profitable to American business. He had, however, respect for the Haitians and an instinct for their sensibilities that was lacking in white American businessmen and naval officers.

Douglass shared with other Afro-Americans a special regard for the Haitians, whose revolution in 1803 succeeded in throwing off both the yokes of slavery and European masters at once. It had managed to survive for nearly a century as a black republic despite the hostility and avarice of European powers.

For sixty years of Haiti's independent existence, the United States had been a powerful northern slave nation, offering asylum for those emigrés who fled Haiti. It had been a hostile neighbor, refusing to offer formal recognition or establish diplomatic relations until 1864. That history was firmly in Douglass's mind. He wanted to do nothing to demean these people, and he believed, or he pretended to believe, that his government shared that sentiment.

The government of President Modestin Hyppolite was in office on Douglass's arrival, having recently come to power through a coup d'état. The previous government of François Legitime had enjoyed the support of European powers, but the United States had backed Hyppolite. It was understood that the conspicuous presence of United States warships in Haitian waters and ports at the time of the coup guaranteed Hyppolite's success, and there was confusion as to whether promises had been made to gain American support. The Americans expected to benefit by the new government at any rate, and many Haitians suspected that the new government was going to make illegal concessions to the United States. Throughout the Douglass ministry the Hyppolite government remained precarious and cautious in its dealing with Americans.

Such was the political atmosphere in which Douglass was asked to assist in two delicate negotiations with the Haitian government. The first was to support an effort to gain for an American mercantile firm, William P. Clyde and Company, special shipping concessions as well as a subsidy from the

Haitian government. The second was to obtain for the United States a lease of Môle St. Nicholas as a naval base and coaling station.

The agent for the Clyde Company asked Douglass to intercede in his behalf with Anténor Firmin, foreign minister of Haiti. Douglass did that willingly, but the agent became impatient as the matter dragged on; he pressed Douglass more. Douglass was to have a special audience with President Hyppolite, and Clyde's agent urged him to take that occasion to bring the trading issue to the president's attention. It was inappropriate, Douglass thought, so he refused, angering the American businessman. After months in which the matter languished, Mr. Firmin informed Clyde's agent that Haiti could not make the desired concessions which might invite other Americans with similar interests to press them through the consul-general. Hoping to counter this objection, the agent asked Douglass to assure Firmin that he would press no other claims of Americans if Haiti would agree to this deal.

Douglass was shocked by the proposal and told the agent so. His office, as he saw it, was to serve the legitimate interests of all United States citizens. He refused flatly to engage in what he called a "shameful" proposal. Favoring the interests of certain businessmen in return for ample considerations had become standard practice among political office holders, and doubtless the agent expected Douglass to be open to such cooperation. Douglass's sense of rectitude made it impossible to entertain such thoughts, and the moral tone of his refusal undoubtedly angered the agent all the more. The results, however, were reports of the incident in the American press which were very unfavorable to Douglass.

The failure to negotiate a lease of Môle St. Nicholas was a more serious problem because it would seem to reflect on Douglass's ability, and thus the ability of any black man, to serve his country's interests abroad. The American press and white Americans had their doubts, that much was certain. From the way President Harrison and his Secretary of State

James G. Blaine handled the matter, they had their doubts as well.

In January 1891 the commander of the North Atlantic fleet, Admiral Bancroft Gherardi, arrived at Port-au-Prince. Rather than present himself to the consulate, as protocol required, Gherardi summoned the minister to meet him aboard his flagship, *Philadelphia.* It was there that Douglass read dispatches from Blaine giving the admiral charge of negotiations for Môle St. Nicholas. Douglass was asked to cooperate in every way that he could. Making no complaint and ignoring the admiral's condescension, Douglass placed himself at Gherardi's service.

The two presented themselves to President Hyppolite and Minister Firmin, and the conversations began. The admiral did all of the talking. Contrary to Douglass's advice, Gherardi stressed what he held to be the Hyppolite government's obligation to the United States. The presence of its warships during the recent coup had been instrumental in its success, and Gherardi claimed that promises had been made. Douglass urged the lease on the grounds that it would help cement good relations between the two countries.

The Haitians denied Gherardi's claim of obligation. Firmin said that such a lease with the United States, at that time, would provoke a revolution. President Hyppolite, however, agreed to submit the matter to his cabinet. Formal written application for a lease of the Môle was made to the Haitian government on 2 February 1891. The document was over Admiral Gherardi's signature, and the minister-resident–consul-general had not been asked to sign.

Taking advantage of the American's thoughtlessness and playing for time, Firmin asked to see the official authorization giving the admiral power to negotiate a treaty for the United States; Gherardi had none. The minister explained the impossibility of his government engaging in a treaty with a person lacking clear and specific authorization to sign for the United States. It was a clever move. Gherardi was tempted to force the issue, but Douglass persuaded him he had no choice but to cable Washington for the necessary documents.

Two months passed before the credentials arrived at Port-au-Prince, during which time Haiti was alive with rumors that the United States planned to take the port by force. Gherardi held his revised powers until April 18, when four American warships steamed into the harbor. Backed by this awesome display of power, and against Douglass's vigorous objections, the admiral presented his new credentials for Firmin demanding Haiti's immediate answer.

In his only official action critical of the admiral, Douglass cabled Blaine to inform him of the dire consequences likely to come from such a flagrant display of power when everyone knew negotiations were going on. He reported the general "feeling of apprehension, anxiety and even of alarm," beyond anything he had previously seen there. "Fear is expressed," he said, "that if . . . the Môle St. Nicholas be ceded or leased to us, the Government that makes the concession will fall under the crash of popular condemnation; that if . . . [it] be not granted, the Môle may be seized by our naval forces now here, and that in either case internal disorders, violence and revolutionary uprisings will follow."

On 22 April 1891, a day following the date of Douglass's dispatch, Haiti formally refused the American request. Firmin's reason put great stress on the presence of warships in Port-au-Prince. It made, he said, "a most unfortunate impression on the entire country. . . . Haiti could not enter negotiations without appearing to yield to foreign pressure and to compromise [de facto] existence as an independent people."

Actually, Haitian intelligence in Washington had learned that President Harrison had no intention of using force to get Môle St. Nicholas, thus Anténor Firmin acted with assurance. On 27 April, Admiral Gherardi withdrew his ships from Haitian waters; his bluff had been called.

The Haitians would have denied the lease under the best of circumstances, but the bumbling and clumsy American effort made matters easy. Douglass's role, except perhaps for being too cooperative with Gherardi, seems to have been honorable enough. He had, however, been set up in such a way that any credit for success would have gone to the admiral and any blame for failure would have fallen on him. Soon after the breakdown of the talks the American newspapers were filled with a version of the story which must have come from Gherardi or his friends in the navy.

Douglass requested a sixty-day leave of absence to spend the months of August and September at home. He claimed the tropical climate was hard on him and he had to get relief. That was true enough, but he was also anxious to tell his side of the story. He resigned his post on 30 July 1891. Harrison and Blaine, probably ambivalent about his appointment from the first, accepted his resignation on August 11.

Douglass gave "personal considerations" as his reason for leaving the office. He remarked that he had aged more during his two years in Haiti than he had in five at home. More than these "personal" matters, however, was his desire to clear his name.

Douglass told his story in a series of newspaper and magazine articles. His critics immediately charged him with revealing diplomatic secrets, but he was unperturbed. He was careful not to display any irrationality, anger or meanness of character. He had played his part without thought of self or race. He was only insistent on honesty and fairness. Both he and the nation's honor had been victimized by individuals and interests that were both racially prejudiced and unscrupulous. He was studiously fair in his treatment of Gherardi, using much the same tone as he had used in describing the characters of the Anthonys and the Aulds, the slavemasters of his youth. He would not attack but let the truth condemn them.

At seventy-five, Douglass was more aware than ever that his life story was his legacy to history. He brought his autobiography up to date; *The Life and Times of Frederick Douglass* included those last years. Here was the stunning blow of the Supreme

Court in the *Civil Rights* cases; here was his marriage to Helen Pitts and his observations of the Old World; here was his record of public service and especially his ministry to Haiti. He had to set the record straight in his own terms, knowing that others would have their say, shaping history to their own design. He was pleased with the "scrupulous justice" done him in the recent biography by Frederick May Holland, but there would be other accounts where he would probably fall under "the keen edge of censure." In the end it would come out right: "Truth is patient and time is just." With this philosophy he could remain content as long as his voice was part of the record.

The embarrassment of the Haitian experience jolted Douglass from his complacency. Despite all that his life had meant, despite his offices and presumed regard within the Republican party, he could be humiliated by Admiral Gerhardi, a white man, and find little sympathy within the government or the public at large. It was a rude reminder of his elemental identity with all other black Americans. While he had never ceased being their champion, he had come to take himself seriously as their exemplar and model. Now, in the aftermath of Haiti, a sharply critical edge returned to his voice. Once more, in the last years of his life, he became the morally enraged "outsider."

The World's Columbian Exposition, which was held in Chicago in 1893, provided Douglass with the platform he needed. The Haitian government, with a clear deliberateness, appointed him their commissioner to the exposition. Douglass understood the gesture: it was the Haitian government's signal to the American people of their high regard for him. Douglass considered it the supreme honor of his life. Indeed, Douglass was to be the only Afro-American to have an official role at the exposition, for the planners studiously avoided blacks in all their appointments. The United States may not in fact have been a white man's country, but this exhibition of American civilization at the century's end would make it seem so.

Blacks had hoped to gain an appointment as commissioner, perhaps, or to membership on a committee of the exposition. As it turned out, there was not a guide or even a guard who was black. They published a protest pamphlet, and Douglass wrote the introduction. It was the old Douglass again. He would reveal to the world that which white Americans would prefer to leave hidden from view. Blacks were the nation's embarrassment, not because they were poor and backward, but because they belied by their oppressed condition American pretensions to civilization, Christianity, and democracy. He would expose that hypocrisy.

The pamphlet was an exposé of outrages perpetrated on blacks; a revelation that lynchings and mob violence remained the lot of the free Southern black man. Much that had seemed gained by blacks as a result of the war was fast being lost due to Afro-American powerlessness against such violence and the indifference of the national government. This was the America that was not on exhibit in Chicago.

If Americans had reason to be proud of their exposition, Douglass stood with other blacks to remind the nation and the world that white Americans in their pride of success had "cause for repentance as well as complaisance . . . for shame as well as glory."

If black Americans could not be officially represented, Douglass would use the office Haiti had provided him to speak both for his own people and those who appointed him. It was not difficult, as he saw it, for they were as one people, with analogous experiences and similar histories. The Haitian, "by reason of ancestral identity," was important to the Afro-American, his history of struggle for freedom more meaningful because "the Negro, like the Jew, can never part with his identity and race." For Douglass race had become the irreducible determinant. No matter what, he said, "the Negro . . . is identified with and shares the fortunes of his race." His lecture retold that parallel history as one of revolutionary struggle against the "progressive, aggressive, all-conquering white man."

Until Haiti struck for freedom, "the Christian world slept profoundly over slavery. It was scarcely troubled even by a dream of this crime against justice and liberty." The mission of Haiti to the world was to shock it into moral consciousness and awaken it to the true character of the black man. As if in ominous reminder to Americans, white and black, Douglass stressed a "grand initial fact: *that the freedom of Haiti was not given as a boon, but conquered as a right!* Her people fought for it."

The parallel between his own people and the Haitians was close in his mind, and that gave him some glimmer of hope. As an assertion of faith in the future, he reminded his audience that Haiti had been boycotted and ostracized by the Christian world for most of its history, but "Haiti still lives." She had made much progress in the last twenty years, attaching itself to "the world's civilization." "I will not, I cannot believe," he said, "that her star will go out in the darkness, but . . . like the star of the North, will shine on and shine on forever."

The realities of post-Reconstruction were bitter for a man whose days were numbered and whose entire life had been governed by a faith in the rightness of his cause. From his youthful conversion to Christianity, his defiant teaching of Bible classes to slaves, of Sunday school in his first days as a free man, Douglass had moved without conscious or deliberate decision from adherence to orthodox Christian doctrine to a faith in a transcendental deity. God was in life, in the forces of history. Divinity was a part of every man and woman, white and black. History, the past forming and shaping the future, was the divinity writ out in time. It was his faith that however slow the wheels ground, they went forward and not backward. The steps the black man had made from slavery were real advances, and they could be built on. Never would he have thought that it would all turn back.

That was, however, what he was being forced to see in his last years. He had ignored or minimized the significance of earlier signs: the growing disinterest in blacks by Northern liberals, the ease with which black political power could be compromised, the splits within the Republican party and its duplicity with regard to blacks, the return of conservative governments in the South, the Supreme Court's erosion of constitutional guarantees of black citizenship rights. He had seen it all happening, commented on most of it, but he had refused to accept it as evidence that the course of the black man in America was running backward.

After his return from Europe in 1888, Douglass had traveled to South Carolina and Georgia. Except for a visit to New Orleans, he had never before ventured south of Virginia. He saw for himself how the sharecropping system held blacks in virtual peonage to their former masters. He was deeply shaken by the poverty, the sense of hopelessness and powerlessness. Only a decade earlier South Carolina had blacks in its legislature and a radical Republican government. But blacks had been able to salvage little after the counterrevolution of Southern whites.

Everywhere in the South, the hard-won franchise had been taken from blacks. Where harassment and violence were not used, legal devices were invented. Mississippi led the way in 1890 by calling a constitutional convention for the avowed purpose of disenfranchising blacks. They designed a new suffrage law that required a two-dollar poll tax, excluding as voters those convicted of bribery, burglary, theft, or bigamy, and barring anyone who could not read any section of the state constitution or understand it when read aloud. Aside from the poll tax itself, this last interpretive feature placed such discretion in the hands of white election officials that 123,000 blacks in Mississippi were wiped off the voter rolls almost overnight. Other Southern states followed the example.

Douglass would not live to see the ultimate refinement in the art of disenfranchisement. In 1898 Louisiana introduced the "grandfather clause," which provided for the permanent registration of all men whose fathers or grandfathers had been qualified to vote as of 1 January 1867—just before the First Reconstruction Act mandated the black vote. While Douglass would not live to see all of it, he was aware in 1893 that a powerful reactionary force had set in. Blacks were without political power and effective citizenship in the South, and the Republican party would do nothing to protect them.

Shattering, too, was the especially ugly turn that Southern violence against blacks had taken. Always deploring the lawlessness of Southern whites, their Klan and vigilante groups, he had assumed it a reaction to the freedmen's attempts to exercise political power. But as Southern whites reclaimed that power, and as blacks ceased to be actual contenders, the violence continued. Now, however, it was in the form of lynch mobs hanging, shooting, burning, and mutilating black men on the charge that they had raped or attempted to rape white women. The sexual aspect of this charge was especially disturbing, for when white Southerners had attacked black men as potential political or economic competitors they were attacking men, however lawlessly and brutally. The lynch mobs, however, raising the specter of sex and lust, were converting their victims into animals in the public's mind. Douglass could see all around him, well-meaning Northern white men and women whose sensibilities were so shocked by the very thought of rape that they abandoned skepticism of the charge and moral offense at the crime of lynching. The epidemic of lynching, more than anything else, signaled to him how easily Northerners were willing to abandon Southern blacks to the mercy of Southern whites.

The feeble public spirit that sustained the moral crusade which ended slavery could scarcely be found in the 1890s. Northern whites had come to place all questions under the single rubric, the Negro Problem, and most seemed relieved that it appeared a problem for Southerners to solve.

In his last years, whatever sense of personal accomplishment Douglass may have felt was overwhelmed by the knowledge that his great crusade had failed. The American people had succumbed to self-indulging prejudice and had missed their chance to create a national community based on law and justice.

In this frame of mind Douglass was closer in his last years to what he had been on the antislavery platform, seeing evil buried deep in the heart of the nation and using his voice to expose it. He was again the man who had spoken to English and American audiences, pointing an accusing finger at American churches and clergy, government and men of property and standing, crying shame on them as a nation of "man stealers" and "woman debauchers."

In the 1890s he took up the issue of lynching. He joined forces with Mary Church Terrell and Ida Wells Barnett, two black women reformers who would lead the frustrating fight against lynching into the twentieth century. He and Mrs. Terrell visited President Harrison in a vain appeal for support of a federal antilynching law. In June 1894 Douglass wrote an attack on lynching and its defenders for the *North American Review.*

He rejected the rationale justifying lynch mobs, denied the common argument that the better class of Southern white men were not responsible. It was a myth that such men deplored the use of violence against blacks, that an "ignorant mob" was the culprit. If men of property and standing really objected to violence, there would be none. Men of "wealth and respectability" were actually quick to raise the cry of an outrage by a "Negro on some white woman," he charged. Yet for over two hundred years this very class of men had "committed this offense against black women, and the fact excited little attention."

There were critics of his article, Southern and Northern. The former governor of South Carolina, D. H. Chamberlain, told Douglass to use his voice to stamp out the vicious crime of rape rather than deny it. Frances Willard, of the Women's Christian Temperance Union, pleaded with Douglass to understand the white Southerner's problem. "The colored race," she wrote, "multiplies like the locusts of Egypt. The safety of women, of childhood, of the home, is menaced."

Douglass answered them in what was to be his last great essay. "Not a breeze comes to us from the late rebellious states," he said, "that is not tainted and freighted with Negro blood." He turned to write a formal argument on the lynching question. The pamphlet, "The Lesson of the Hour; Why the Negro is Lynched," reached beyond the specific question of lynching and exposed what Douglass saw to be something darker and more foreboding at the heart of American society.

The most notable fact of this new wave of violence was the disintegration of civilized society into mob rule and mob law. More shocking than the fact of violence itself was how easily a Christian society had grown accustomed to it and was no longer offended by the pervading lawlessness against black people. Lynching could not be dismissed as the excesses of ignorant mobs, for with few exceptions, he said, "the upper classes of the South seem to be in full sympathy." The press and pulpit were either silent or openly apologetic. He pointed to the former governor, Chamberlain, and the genteel Frances Willard. Both would normally be considered sane, Christian persons, but they were totally insensible to the moral outrages being committed against blacks. Rather, their hearts ached with pity at the plight of the poor Southern white man, whom they pictured as forced to burn, murder, and mutilate blacks. "What perversity!" Douglass wrote.

Douglass saw in this broad sentimentality a conspiracy to characterize the black man as a monster. The white imagination was willing, indeed anxious, to accuse blacks of any enormity. It was a well-established device of blaming the victim. Whites, from the days of slavery, cleverly sought among blacks the cause for their own exploitation, oppression, and brutalization. Whites could never imagine themselves un-Christian tyrants, but they sought something in the race of blacks which would explain white brutishness to themselves. The lynch mob —the very epitome of un-Christian and uncivilized behavior— had to be the fault of the victim and his race.

Douglass was not deceived. The wave of violence had nothing to do with an actual epidemic of black men violating white women. Two centuries of opportunity, even during the war when Southern white women were most vulnerable, charges of rape by black men were almost unknown. They came now, not because of a miraculous audacity on the part of black men, but as a means of making them beasts in the public mind. Thus, they could not only be deprived of citizenship rights, but all human considerations as well.

Most disturbing to Douglass was how men and women of good will had readily sought wrongheaded accommodations to keep peace with this evil. Many had become discouraged by the ignorance and illiteracy of black voters in the South. Black as well as white men succumbed. Douglass could remember as forceful a black leader as Martin Delany, two decades earlier, being discouraged by the freedmen as voter. Now there were those like the black politician, John M. Langston, who entertained the thought that educational and literacy qualifications —restricting the vote to the educated classes of both races— would be a fair accommodation which would remove whatever reason there might be in complaints against black voters.

Of such men Douglass said, "much learning has made them mad." Because blacks needed education, they needed the ballot: "Take the ballot from the Negro and you take from him all means and motives that make for education." The educated classes could never be depended on to share their advantage with blacks, "especially when they have a fixed purpose to make this entirely a white man's government." He would argue for making the franchise more inclusive rather than more exclusive: "I would not only include the men, but would gladly include the women, and make our government in reality . . . for the whole people."

Those who argued for restricting the franchise by literacy or other tests, explicitly, placed the blame on blacks for the corruption and disorder of postwar Southern politics. In this, too, was a falseness. Blacks had never set up a separate party, nor adopted a "Negro platform," nor sought to lead. They had followed white leaders and supported one or the other major party. In this, they had been no different from the enlightened citizens in the rest of the country. The American people must know that if the major parties have been guided by intelligence and patriotism, so too the black voters who followed them. Whatever the character of American politics, the fault was with the whole American people, not just the blacks, and it was certainly not a question of literacy.

Douglass could not hide his despair at the decay of a national sense of justice and spirit of liberty under what was called the Negro Problem. "I have sometimes thought," he wrote, "that the American people are too great to be small, too just and magnanimous to oppress the weak." His faith in the American future had rested on that belief and fond hope. Now he had doubts.

The "American method" of reasoning about blacks was, as during slavery, to "invert everything; turn truth upside down, and put the case of the unfortunate Negro inside out and wrong end foremost." Thus, the sharecropper was poor and ignorant not because he was oppressed and unfairly exploited, but his condition explained why he was treated unjustly.

The so-called Negro Problem was the best example of this reasoning. Here was the greatest of sophistries, making the "worse appear to be the better reason." By calling the broad phenomenon of injustice to blacks the Negro Problem, one "removes the burden of proof from the old master class and imposes it on the Negro. It puts upon the race a work which belongs to the nation." It places "the fault at the door of the

Negro and removes it from the door of the white man, shields the guilty and blames the innocent, makes the Negro responsible, when it should so make the nation."

The real problem, Douglass insisted, was the race prejudice in the hearts of white people which corrupted the nation. When one saw it that way, the path to solving the problem was clear. If white people in the North and South could conquer their prejudice, if the Northern "press and pulpit" would proclaim the gospel of truth and justice against the war now being made upon the Negro, "if the American people would cultivate kindness and humanity, if the South ceased to unfairly exploit black labor, if white men could give up the deception that they could be free while making the Negro a slave," they would find the answer. "Let the nation try justice and the problem will be solved."

He had little hope. In the past he had felt he could rely on the Republican party. With all its faults, it had a historical commitment to liberty and the rights of blacks. That too was changed: "The Republican party is converted into a party of money, rather than a party of humanity and justice." To many, Douglass had been slow in coming to see that.

Nothing to him was more ominous than the resuscitation in those ugly days of schemes, long thought dead and buried, to colonize Afro-Americans outside the United States. What made matters worse was that because of racial persecution, black men of "acknowledged ability and learning" were becoming advocates. Douglass's mind was no different from what it had been in the 1840s and 1850s. It was a pernicious and cruel deception. The expense and hardships connected with the removal of any sizeable portion of the Afro-American population made any such scheme impractical: "The American people are wicked, but they are not fools."

For those blacks and whites now advocating colonization, his judgment was as clear and uncluttered as it had always been. He was willing to grant that they might mean well, but little more: "If they are sensible, they are insincere; and if they are sincere, they are not sensible." He himself objected to any plan that would weaken the black man's hold on one country while giving him no rational hope of belonging to another. If the American people "could endure the Negro's presence while a slave, they certainly can and ought to endure his presence as a free man." But all such arguments for and against colonization were pointless: "We are here and are here to stay. It is well for us and well for the American people to rest upon this as final."

"The Lesson of the Hour" was in fact Douglass's valedictory. The old man, in his despair and disillusionment, had reached back and rediscovered the younger man's vision, fire, and ideals. It was abolitionism all over again, foreshadowing the struggle for justice that Afro-Americans would be forced to make through the next seventy-five years.

On 20 February 1895 Frederick Douglass died. He was seventy-seven years old, but he did not know for certain. People who were born slaves seldom had a birth date—day or year. They might not even have had known parents or kin, and certainly they had no birthright. Douglass had lived to make birthright claims for himself, his children, and his people. In death, like Lincoln, he stood for an essence in the national ideal yet to be realized. He died an honored man.

It had been a typical day. He attended the morning sessions of the National Council of Women, meeting in Washington. He returned to Cedar Hill, and while he was acting out some events of the day for Helen Douglass, he fell dead of a heart attack.

After memorial services at the Metropolitan African Methodist Episcopal Church, his body was transported to Rochester. There it lay in state at the City Hall, and on February 26 he was buried at the Mount Hope Cemetery in Rochester. Black Americans, and white Americans too, would mourn the passing of a great American. All seemed to know that with his death an era had passed away.

On 18 September 1895 just seven months after Douglass's death, another black man who had also been born a slave stood before a mainly white audience in Atlanta, Georgia. Much of what Booker T. Washington said, Frederick Douglass would have applauded. He would have liked the emphasis on the need for blacks to obtain industrial skills. He would have heard the call for whites and blacks to "cast down your buckets where you are" as an eloquent plea against emigration and colonization. He would have said a loud amen to the notion that the future of the South—its prosperity or its depression—would depend on the mutual respect and cooperation between blacks and whites.

With all of that, however, he would have deplored Washington's speech: the tone, the apology, the deference. How strange to imply that it had been a mistake to give political power to freedmen, to deliver so willingly the control and leadership of the South to white men. How contrary to experience for black men to rely on the good will of white men. How peculiar for a black leader to promise no "artificial forcing," to deny any claim to "social equality." How cowardly to ignore the existence of those great postwar amendments, abandoning just claims for citizenship.

Washington accepted what was, segregation included. "In all things that are purely social we can be as separate as the fingers, yet one as the hand in all things essential to mutual progress." Such was the language of the black leader who would cast his shadow over American race relations for the next twenty-five years. Given the state of things, perhaps no other kind of black leadership could have been effective. In that sense Douglass's death did mark the end of an era.

If so, it was a tough reality that Douglass was mercifully spared. In the year following his death and Washington's ascendance, after all, the Supreme Court in *Plessy* v. *Ferguson* resurrected the "separate but equal" doctrine, smothering any last feeble hopes of a "new national era" in which black people would be full citizens in the nation.

In 1899 a young man asked Booker T. Washington what he would advise for a young, black man starting into the new century. Washington's answer was characteristic: "Work! Work! Work! Be patient and win by superior service." The same young man had asked Douglass the very same question less than a month before he died. The old man's answer came from the entirety of his life: "Agitate! Agitate! Agitate!" Far into the twentieth century, black Americans would testify that one bit of advice was of little use without the other.

# A Note on the Sources

Students of Frederick Douglass should look first at his own writings about himself. He wrote three major autobiographies, each succeeding the earlier by at least a decade, apparently merely bringing his story up to date. Careful comparison, however, reveals subtle but significant changes in his telling about his life. These autobiographies are instructive about both the man and his use of history: *The Narrative of the Life of Frederick Douglass, an American Slave, Written by Himself* (1845); *My Bondage and My Freedom* (1855); and *The Life and Times of Frederick Douglass* (1881). Frederick Douglass's papers are being published by Yale University Press under the editorship of John W. Blassingame. The first volume was scheduled to appear in 1979 but was not in print as this book went to press.

The research efforts of Mr. Dickson J. Preston in the plantation and county records of Talbot County, Maryland, have uncovered considerable new information about the young Frederick Douglass and his family. Among other things, we are for the first time certain that Douglass's birth was in 1818, rather than 1817 as he believed. Mr. Preston is presently writing a book based on this material and expects to publish it in 1981.

Douglass became the subject of biographies as the nineteenth century closed. Frederic May Holland, *Frederick Douglass* (1891) is a reflection by an abolitionist. Charles W. Chesnutt, the notable black novelist, wrote his *Frederick Douglass* in 1899.

It took another fifty years before major scholarly biographies appeared. Benjamin Quarles's *Frederick Douglass* (1948) is solid and careful. Philip S. Foner's four-volume *The Life and Writings of Frederick Douglass* (1950–1955) is invaluable in that it comprises both biography and selected speeches, essays, and letters by Douglass. The forthcoming Yale edition of Douglass's papers promises to be comprehensive in documents, but it will not completely supplant these handy volumes edited by Foner. Quarles himself edited a one-volume collection of Douglass's speeches and writings in *Frederick Douglass* (1968).

It is necessary to go beyond the story of the man. There are several excellent histories explaining the world he lived in. Leon Litwack, *North of Slavery: The Negro in the Free States, 1790–1860* (1961); Eugene Berwanger, *The Frontier Against Slavery: Western Anti-Negro Prejudice and the Slavery Extension Controversy* (1967); V. Jacque Voegeli, *Free but Not Equal: the Middle West and the Negro During the Civil War* (1967); and Eric Foner, *Free Soil, Free Labor, Free Men: The Ideology of the Republican Party Before the Civil War* (1970), give the best general picture of the political and social realities for antebellum Northern blacks. Constance M. Green, *A History of Race Relations in the Nation's Capital* (1967), has chapters covering the antebellum period as well as those years of Douglass's residency. Leonard Sweet, *Black Images of America, 1784–1870* (1976), is an excellent intellectual history which places Douglass among his black contemporaries, analyzing their notions of nationality. In this regard, Frank A. Rollins's *Life and Public Services of Martin R. Delany* (1885) remains useful as a point of comparison with Douglass's life and thought. Howard H. Bell, *A Survey of the Negro Convention Movement, 1830–1844* (1933), gives a full and descriptive account of that important forum.

Historians of abolitionists, until recently, have not considered the black role sufficiently distinctive to warrant particular analysis. Early works, like Gilbert H. Barnes's *The Anti-Slavery Impulse, 1830–1844* (1933), were mainly preoccupied with distinguishing between Garrison and his antagonists within the movement; and even Aileen Kraditor's *Means and Ends in American Abolitionism: Garrison and His Critics on Strategy and Tactics, 1834–1850* (1969) provides only a corrective to overly critical treatments of Garrison. Recent work, however, has discovered the problem of racism among white abolitionists as well as distinctive objectives among blacks, casting fresh light on Frederick Douglass and his allies. James McPherson, *Struggle For Equality: Abolitionists and the Negro in the Civil War and Reconstruction* (1964), and Martin Duberman, ed., *The Anti-Slavery Vanguard; New Essays on the Abolitionists* (1965), are early fruits of that reconsideration. Benjamin Quarles, *Black Abolitionists* (1969), is the first work that focused on the particular and important role of blacks; it is essential. John H. Bracey, Jr., et al., eds., *Blacks in the Abolitionist Movement* (1971), provides documents. While not supplanting Quarles's work, Jane H. and William H. Pease's *They Who Would Be Free: Blacks' Search for Freedom, 1830–1861* (1974) takes a broader canvas of Afro-American protest and struggle for reform in the antebellum period.

Among the many books on the antislavery movement, some are especially informative about matters of concern to Douglass. Carleton Mabee, *Black Freedom, The Nonviolent Abolitionist from 1830 Through the Civil War* (1970); Peter Walker, *Moral Choices, Memory, Desire, and Imagination in 19th Century Abolition* (1978); Lawrence Lader, *The Bold Brahmins: New England's War against Slavery, 1831–1863* (1961); Leonard L. Richards, *"Gentlemen of Property and Standing": Anti-Abolition Mobs in Jacksonian America* (1970); and P. J. Staudenraus, *The African Colonization Movement, 1816–1865* (1961). The following books about subjects tangent to Douglass's antebellum years are worth attention. Stephen B. Oates, *To Purge This Land with Blood: A Biography of John Brown* (1970), as well as Oates's *Allies For Freedom: Blacks and John Brown* (1974), tell the story of one kind of "direct action," while Larry Gara's *Liberty Line: The Legend of the Underground Railroad* (1961) discusses another.

Slavery was the single most formative institution of Frederick Douglass's life. It has also been subject to major reinterpretation in recent years. Kenneth M. Stampp's *The Peculiar Institution* (1957) remains the best "institutional" study. John W. Blassingame, *The Slave Community* (1972); Eugene D. Genovese, *Roll, Jordan, Roll; The World the Slaves Made* (1974); Herbert G. Gutman, *The Black Family in Slavery and Freedom, 1750–1925* (1976); and Nathan I. Huggins, *Black Odyssey: The Afro-American Ordeal in Slavery* (1977), have shifted the perspective to that of the slave. Special studies have also been important: Ira Berlin, *Slaves Without Masters: The Free Negro in the Antebellum South* (1974); Richard C. Wade, *Slavery in the Cities: The South, 1820–1860* (1964); and Robert S. Starobin, *Industrial Slavery in the Old South* (1970).

Douglass's concerns in the Civil War are illuminated by Benjamin Quarles, *The Negro in the Civil War* (1953); James M. McPherson, *The Negro's Civil War* (1965); and Dudley T. Cornish, *The Sable Arm: Negro Troops in the Union Army, 1861–1865* (1956). There are many excellent local studies of reconstruction. The following books take up general questions of importance to Douglass: James E. Sefton, *Andrew Johnson and the Uses of Constitutional Power* (1980); Carl R. Osthaus, *Freedom, Philanthropy, and Fraud: A History of the Freedman's Savings Bank* (197 ); Nell I. Painter, *Exodusters: Black Migration to Kansas Following Reconstruction* (1977); C. Vann Woodward, *Reunion and Reaction: The Compromise of 1877 and the End of Reconstruction* (1951); Vincent P. De Santis, *Republicans Face the Southern Question, 1877–1897* (1959); Stanley P. Hirshson, *Farewell to the Bloody Shirt: Northern Republicans and the Southern Negro, 1877–1893* (1962), covers the same ground as De Santis but with more emphasis on racial politics; LaWanda and John Cox, *Politics, Principle and Prejudice, 1865–1866: Dilemma of Reconstruction America* (1963). For general discussions of the period, W. E. B. DuBois, *Black Reconstruction, 1860–1880* (1953) is a classic; and Rayford M. Logan, *The Betrayal of the Negro* (1965) is comprehensive.

There are many fine books a student of Frederick Douglass

will find illuminating. John H. Bracey, Jr., et al., eds., *Free Blacks in America, 1800–1860* (1971), is a collection of documents; John W. Blassingame, ed., *Slave Testimony; Two Centuries of Letters, Speeches, Interviews, and Autobiographies* (1977); Carter G. Woodson, *The Education of the Negro Prior to 1861* (1968), was first published in 1915; Thomas L. Webber, *Deep Like the Rivers: Education in the Slave Quarter Community, 1831–1865* (1978); Don E. Fehrenbacher, *The Dred Scott Case* (1978), is the best and fullest treatment of that crucial case; David H. Donald, *Liberty and Union* (1978), as with Professor Donald's other work, leans to the view that the Union was and ought to have been the first consideration in the crisis years of the 1850s; Herman Belz, *Emancipation and Equal Rights: Politics and Constitutionalism in the Civil War Era* (1978); and Leon Litwack, *Been in the Storm So Long: The Aftermath of Slavery* (1979), is a full, extensive, and humane restatement of the transition in the South from slavery to freedom.

Particular topics in reconstruction are taken up in Theodore B. Wilson, *The Black Codes of the South* (1965); James L. Roark, *Masters Without Slaves: Southern Planters in the Civil War and Reconstruction* (1977); George R. Bentley, *A History of the Freedmen's Bureau* (1955); John Eaton, *Grant, Lincoln and the Freedmen with Special Reference to the Work for the Contrabands and Freedmen of the Mississippi Valley* (1969), first published in 1907; Louis S. Gerteis, *From Contraband to Freedmen: Federal Policy Toward Southern Blacks, 1861–1865* (1973); Jacobus ten Broek, *Equality Under the Law* (1965), was originally entitled *The Anti-Slavery Origins of the Fourteenth Amendment.*

Some of the best work on reconstruction focuses on state or local experience. The following are essential to a student of the subject: Willie Lee Rose, *Rehersal for Reconstruction: The Port Royal Experiment* (1964); Joel Williamson, *After Slavery: The Negro in South Carolina During Reconstruction* (1965); Thomas Holt, *Black over White: Negro Political Leadership in South Carolina During Reconstruction* (1978), is one of the best of the recent political studies; Martin Abbott, *The Freedmen's Bureau in South Carolina,*

*1865–1872* (1967); Howard A. White, *The Freedmen's Bureau in Louisiana* (1970); Peyton McCrary, *Abraham Lincoln and Reconstruction, the Louisiana Experiment* (1978) assumes that if Lincoln had a reconstruction program it can be seen in the Louisiana story; Peter C. Ripley, *Slaves and Freedmen in Civil War Louisiana* (1976); Vernon L. Wharton, *The Negro in Mississippi, 1865–1890* (1947), continues to stand up after much new interpretation of the period; Peter Kolchin, *First Freedom: The Response of Alabama Blacks to Emancipation and Reconstruction* (1972); Joe M. Richardson, *The Negro in the Reconstruction of Florida, 1865–1877* (1965); James A. Rawley, *Race and Politics: "Bleeding Kansas" and the Coming of the Civil War* (1969).

The last concerns of Douglass's life had to do with Haiti and the upsurge of violence and lynching in the South. On Haiti, Rayford W. Logan, *The Diplomatic Relations of the United States with Haiti, 1776–1891* (1941), remains definitive; Robert Debs Heinl and Nancy Gordon Heinl, *Written in Blood, The Story of the Haitian People, 1492–1971* (1978), is a recent, general history. There are a few recent, scholarly books on lynching, but the story is told in Frank Shay, *Judge Lynch, His First Hundred Years* (1938); James E. Cutler, NAACP, *Thirty Years of Lynching in the United States, 1889–1918* (1969); and Walter F. White, *Rope and Faggot: A Biography of Judge Lynch* (1969).

# Index